Marcel Nickler

Running the Sanara

PRAISE FOR

RUNNING THE SAHARA

"I was fascinated by how thoroughly Marcel planned and successfully implemented his desert project. He paid attention to every small detail in his equipment and prepared his body as best as he could for the strenuous, long-lasting heat strain. He matured into a fennec fox and mentally managed to transfer the positive and radiate it. Chapeau, Marcel, you earned the biggest gold kudos."

Aeneas Appius, *multiple World, European and Swiss Duathlon champion*

"This is a powerful story about pursuing your dreams, about stretching your belief, about what is possible and about sitting with your pain when the running gets tough. Marcel's story shows that success is above all, a question of mental strength, dedication, and resilience. It is not so much about beating the others – it is about bringing out the best version of yourself."

Karsten Drath, *executive coach, speaker, author, and around-the-world-cyclist*

"My lasting memory of the Marathon des Sables is one of intense hardship. Coping with the environment in the desert can lead to extreme moments and situations. *Running the Sahara* is a must-read and companion for anybody thinking about signing up for this grueling adventure."

Sir Ranulph Fiennes, *explorer, writer and poet*

Marcel Nickler

Running the Sahara

A diary from the desert and beyond

© 2019 Marcel Nickler

with Scott Solano

Cover design: Domo Loew

All rights reserved. This book or any portion thereof may not be reproduced or used in any manner whatsoever without the express written permission of the publisher except for the use of brief quotations in a book review.

Production and publishing: BoD – Books on Demand, Norderstedt

ISBN: 978-3-7504-2315-2

I dedicate this book to my wife, Monika.
Without her support, I would not have been able
to make my dreams come true.

PREFACE

"Life is too short to waste time on second-class ambitions. Go for the big ones, even if that means a higher failure rate." This famous quote is by Sir Ranulph Fiennes, known as the world's last living explorer. I had the pleasure of meeting Ranulph in 2011 at a global partner meeting of our firm, where he held a memorable and inspiring keynote with the title "Beyond the Limits." Because I was in charge of organizing the meeting, I was lucky enough to have a couple of interactions with him. And looking back, that was a crucial moment in preparing me for something bigger. The Marathon des Sables? Though I didn't have it in mind at that time, I am sure Ranulph's anectodes about his time in the desert influenced me. And interestingly, we also shared some of our running experiences, as he and I had both finished the Ultra Trail du Mont Blanc and the Swissalpine Marathon.

At the starting line in the Moroccan desert, writing a book about my adventure was not even a thought. The idea developed in the months after my return to Switzerland when I was encouraged by some of my colleagues who listened to stories I told about it.

In August 2017, I met Scott Solano for the first time in Frankfurt, and he became somewhat of a mentor for this book. Though the first chapter may have taken longer than initially planned, it was clear to me from the very beginning that quality was more important than adhering to a given time line. It was more important at that stage to find the right tone and pace and set the scene for the book.

At some points, writing was quite an emotional journey for me, when, for example, I tried to describe some crucial moments I faced in the past. During the process of writing, I reflected on some things and moments in my life that I even seemed to keep hidden from myself, locking them away in the undeserved background. It was an incredibly intense exercise, and I am glad I didn't miss out on it.

Running the Sahara is the result of a two-year journey that I enjoyed very much. During that time, I learned a lot about myself, and some parts of the book surprised me when I recalled them. The human brain forgets quickly, and writing is an excellent way to force oneself to examine essential and intimate aspects of one's life.

I wish you a good read and hope that you enjoy it. Any feedback on the book is more than welcome, and I'm happy to answer personally every incoming mail I get at marcel@runningthesahara.net.

ACKNOWLEDGMENTS

I have to start by thanking my wonderful wife, Monika. She was the one who encouraged me to sign up for the adventure in the Sahara, and her mental support was just unbelievable in all phases of the book project. That also included reading early drafts and pieces as well as giving me advice on the cover and the design of the book. She was as important in getting this book done as I was.

After some time of reflection around my crazy idea of running the Marathon des Sables, I gained the full buy-in of my daughters, Manuela and Simone, and they both were indispensable and important companions.

Writing a book is harder than I thought and more rewarding than I could have ever imagined. All of this wouldn't have been possible without the help and great support of my mentor Scott Solano. I learned a lot about storytelling from him, which added substantial value to this book.

I would also like to thank everyone who made themselves available as a sparring partner when discussing the book, and I hope that I didn't steal too much of your precious time. You know who you are.

And last but not least, a big thanks to everybody who helped me in getting prepared as best as possible for the unknown: Aeneas, Anke, Birgit, Brigitte, Marco, Markus, my coach Timon, and all those not specifically named.

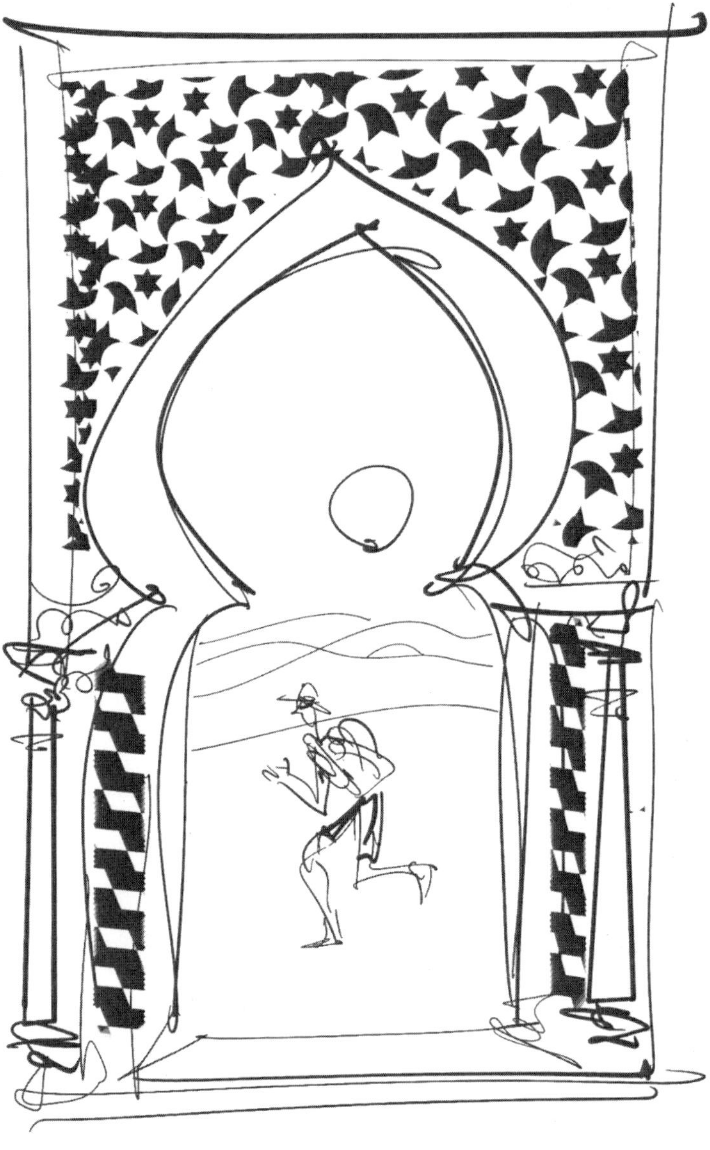

CONTENTS

Stage One – Beyond Imagination
21

Herr Hammermann
25

A Person's Currency
31

Stage One – To the Bivouac
33

Emergence of an Idea
37

Stage Two – String of Pearls
43

Preparation and Equipment
49

Stage Three – Call of the Berbers
57

Arrival in Morocco
65

Stage Four – Steps Ahead
75

Ultramarathon
83

Stage Four – Nightfall
89

The Bivouac Experience
95

Stage Five – Highway to Hell
103

Notes on Running
111

Stage Six – Running for a Cause
119

Epilogue
127

Picture Moments
133

Equipment List
149

Food List
157

Marathons and More
165

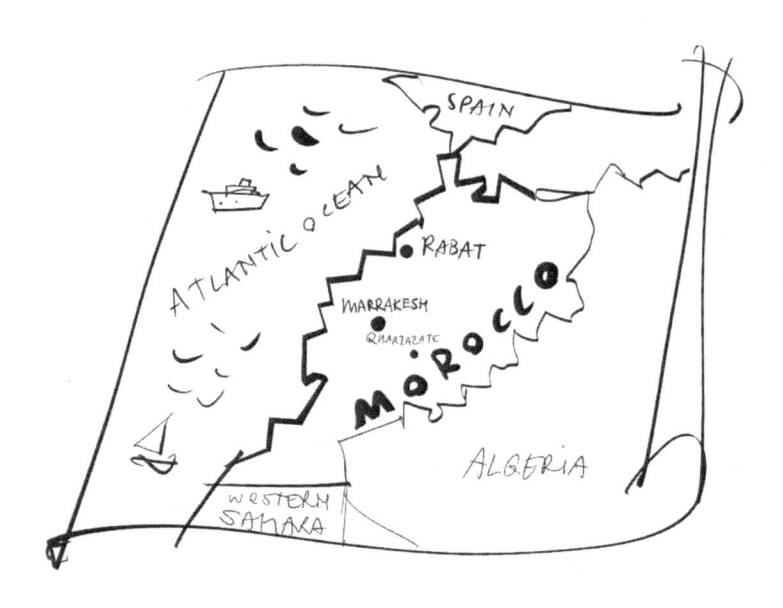

TIMGALINE
to
WEST AGUENOUN N'OUMERHIOUT

STAGE ONE

BEYOND IMAGINATION

Flowing.

A river through the desert.

The body moves over the ground. Undulating muscles make a rhythm for the beating heart and aspirations, and my breath and my shoes hitting the sand are the only audible instruments as I flow through the dunes. Time has been left behind.

The morning heat has brought out a sheen of perspiration on my skin; my body feels like a well-oiled machine. I am 10 kilometers in on the first day of the 32nd Marathon des Sables. Any doubts or fears I may have had about the race have been dispelled.

I am flowing through the desert, near euphoric, overwhelmed by nature. There is a line of small dunes on either side of me, and towering, majestic dunes off to my left. The sky is vast, and an open horizon holds no secrets for kilometers.

This is fun, and the fun is set to continue for another six days. I and nearly 1,200 other participants are attempting to cross 237 kilometers of the Sahara Desert in southeastern Morocco. The Marathon des Sables is one of the world's most grueling races, and I know that many people regard what I'm doing as insanity, but all I'm feeling right now is joy, something like the ecstasy whirling dervishes or congregations with raised and waving hands shouting praise must feel. I could do a few whirls too, but besides joy, there's something else I'm feeling: thirst.

I check my watch and see that it's well over 15 minutes since I took my last swallow of water. The beauty of the moment had captured me. I am carefully monitoring my water intake to make sure I have a few sips every quarter of an hour. I started the race with 1.5 liters of water divided between the two bottles attached to the front shoulder straps of my backpack with a straw in each for easy intake. Depending on the stage, I'll get one or two 1.5-liter PET bottles at every checkpoint during the race and use the first bottle to fill up the shoulder strap bottles. The second bottle I'll affix to the top of my front pack. I swallow two tablets of salt with the first sip from an opened PET bottle to give me the electrolytes I'll need to keep my body going. It is morning and relatively cool, only around 20 degrees Celsius, though I'm still losing water and salt through my sweat. But it is nothing compared to what I will be losing when the sun makes the desert a blazing oven, pushing the temperature over 40 degrees Celsius, which will be baking all the moisture out of me in only a few minutes. I will be drinking water every 5 minutes by then.

If you are unfamiliar with the ultramarathon scene, then you probably believe people who run them are insane, and in a way, I'd agree, we are. People often ask me why I do it, why I would push my body and mind to their breaking points, and the simple answer I usually give is, "Because I can."

Of course, there is much more to why I run than that.

At the starting line today, there were people from all over the world and all walks of life. Scientists are running, engineers, doctors, mothers, people searching for a path. Some were in costumes, and one man was even strumming a ukulele and singing, and it looked like he would be strumming and singing throughout the race. Yes, maybe many of us are somewhat crazy, but all of us are also connected: we are all runners who want to push ourselves past the impossible.

All of us have done a lot of preparation for this race, and maybe I am romanticizing or projecting onto the other runners what I consider to be one of my greatest strengths – and running has helped me to attain it – and that is balance. I sensed at the starting line that all of us had a certain balance, and if we didn't have it, we wouldn't be running this race, let alone finishing it.

The story I am telling as you run with me in the desert is not so much about running as it is about what running has given me and what I've discovered about myself and life through running. Much of it is about where the pounding of my feet has taken me in my thoughts and how I have applied what running has gifted me.

I am not a runner fighting for championships, so don't expect tales of my duels with the world's best ultrarunners. I grew up in Basel, Switzerland, and not Copper Canyon in northern Mexico with the Tarahumara. I have run two sub-3-hour marathons – a feat many healthy people could probably reach with the right training and discipline, and if they start young enough … and have a bit of luck – and though time was important to me because I had set myself the goal of breaking 3 hours, the greatest race for me has no clock, and that race has always been the one with myself. It took me many years to realize that. Some of the lessons I have learned from running long distances are that difficult phases can be overcome, that difficulties and pain are teachers, and you come out as a better and stronger person, or at least I hope I have.

I take a few sips of water as my feet pick their way over an *oued*, a dried riverbed of packed sand and rocks. I had heard that running on these dried riverbeds can be brutal, that it can feel as if the sand and stones beat the energy out of your calves, but here at around kilometer 10, all is going well.

The small dunes on either side are wondrously sculpted, and the towering dunes off to the left are so magnificent that it is almost difficult for me to accept that they are there, that they are not from my imagination. I would not be surprised seeing T. E. Lawrence atop one of the dunes scanning the desert with his camera. It is a magical setting, and there is a softness to the harsh landscape.

It is said that you can sometimes hear the dunes singing. Wind moving over the dunes creates overhangs of sand, and when an overhang eventually collapses, it triggers an avalanche of grains of sand. Amazingly, grains of sand sing at different frequency levels depending on the region. While Moroccan dunes sing in the neighborhood of G-sharp (two octaves below the middle C), the Omani sands may cover frequencies between F-sharp and D. I haven't heard the dunes singing yet, but I hope that I will before the race ends.

Water and salt are going to save me today, and I better not get too distracted by the beauty around me, by the seductress that is Mother Nature. Even though the first day is the "introductory" run, a relatively short jaunt of 30.3 kilometers, the first day always sees a few unfortunate souls already having to drop out. I would bet that at least one person who won't run after today didn't drink enough water.

I cannot recollect if I was thinking about it while entranced by the dunes around kilometer 10 on that first day, but it's a good place to pretend I was and talk about something I've thought a lot about on many of my runs. Though I am an executive at a large consultancy, money has never been what has driven me, and I never judge a person by what is in his or her *Portemonnaie*.

What is a person's currency?

HERR HAMMERMANN

Like all great teachers, running has seemingly unlimited patience. It is always there waiting for you, whether you want it to be or not, and some mornings when the bed is warm and Sirens beckon from the land of sleep, you may wish you had Socrates and his dialectic instead of the command to move.

My passion for long-distance running started in 1998 after a friend of mine, Tobias Scheuring, told me about the incredible experience he had running a marathon. Up to that point, I had participated in some races, a few 10Ks and half marathons, but running was more a way to keep in shape than a passion, than a way of life. I was more into cycling back then, but it did not have a hold on me or even come close to giving me what running has.

Listening to Tobias talk about the marathon – and he had chosen the Lausanne Marathon to be his first – inspired me to give it a go. Though the Lausanne Marathon is not a big name when it comes to marathons, not like Boston, New York, London, and Berlin, it is undoubtedly one of the most beautiful in the world. It starts in the city of Lausanne and follows the shore of Lake Geneva and alongside the Lavaux Vineyard Terraces, which are in UNESCO's World Heritage List. Running in such a setting, as Tobias described it, with hundreds of runners becoming part of the city and the amazing landscape with the finish at the Olympic Museum, made me want my first marathon to be in Lausanne too. What made me want to run even more than the setting, though, was what Tobias had said about the physical and mental challenges of running such a distance.

I had run a few half marathons, but I had never "hit the wall" because I had never run far enough. After listening to Tobias relate his sensations of hitting the wall and his struggle to push past it, I knew that I had to experience the hammer coming down on the body. I have always enjoyed challenges, and the transition from when the body burns up all its carbohydrates and switches to using predominantly body fat for fuel, as crazy as it may sound, was something I needed to experience. Challenging myself has always been what has kept me going, and that applies to my professional life as well.

I did not immediately start waking up early and go running because that is not how I go about things. For good or bad – and I would argue much to my benefit, for it is how I enjoy going about things – I first researched running marathons and prepared a training plan and set a goal for myself, which was to finish the marathon in 3 hours and 30 minutes. Looking back at that time, I see how much the world has changed in the last two decades. I was not searching the internet but was flipping through magazines and books searching for the best information on how to prepare for a marathon. The book I found, written by Thomas Steffens and Martin Grüning, had just recently been issued by Runner's World. It included a systematic plan for successfully running a marathon at different target times, and that was the perfect approach for me. When I have a goal, I always make a plan on how to reach it, and I stick to the plan. I would say that it is one of my strengths.

My wife Monika and I saw the marathon as a daring goal but not something that would turn into the passion that it is today, or that I would someday push myself to even longer distances. The plan called for four training sessions per week, with long runs on the weekend every two weeks. Our daughters, Manuela and Simone, were still small, and with the help of Monika, I was able to have time for the runs and still pursue my professional obligations and duties.

As the day of the marathon drew near, I could feel my adrenaline levels spiking. I was nervous at times, and now and again, a voice in my head would ask what the hell I was doing. But I was mostly excited, and the training had gone well. I had only missed a couple of training sessions at most and felt confident that I would conquer the marathon.

Tobias would be with me for my first marathon. We took the train from Basel to Lausanne the day before the race and checked into a hotel by the lake in Lausanne Ouchy. After picking up our bib numbers, we left our own drink bottles to be distributed along the racecourse as you can do at some marathons, and that allowed me to use my proven sports drink. It was a little thing, but when you add up little things, like loose change, you can purchase something, and in this case, I was buying a psychological boost. Perhaps that boost would be there when I needed it most.

We had decided to pass on mountains of pasta at the pasta party and instead chose to dine at a cozy restaurant in the old part of town. Some runners may frown, but of course we raised glasses of a fine red wine and made a toast to a strong race. A glass of red wine helps get a better night's sleep. It is also said that the penultimate night before a race is more critical, and I had slept well in my own bed beside my wife.

The body should have at least 3 hours to get going before the start of a race, so I had set my alarm clock for 6:00 a.m. and had also asked my wife to call me just in case. A third hedge was the wake-up service of the hotel. That may sound a bit over the top and probably is, but putting the little things in place gives me the certainty that what I can control will not go wrong.

My internal clock has proven to be extremely reliable. I seldom need an alarm clock, having never really overslept in my life, and I actually woke up in Lausanne a few minutes before the programmed alarm. I switched off the alarm clock before the shrill beeping would have started and happily picked up the call from Monika, who once again gave me her best wishes for a successful run. The hotel wake-up service had forgotten to call.

I then followed the procedure that I have used in all my marathons. I put on my running clothes that I had laid out the night before, with the bib number already neatly pinned to the front of my shirt, and I took my body out for a short, easy run to get the engine going and up to operating temperature. I took a light breakfast with Tobias, just as I would at home, keeping to my comfort zone, and then we went back to our rooms. For half an hour, I relaxed by listening to music: Bruce Springsteen was my favorite choice at the time.

About an hour before the start, Tobias and I slowly made our way to the Place de Milan for the nine o'clock start. Other runners were also making their way to the start, and there would be almost 1,500 of us running, and many would probably also be running their first marathon. The weather was as expected: a blue sky, nearly no wind, about 10 degrees Celsius. It would be optimal running conditions. In general, 12 degrees Celsius is the ideal temperature for running a marathon, with deviations above and below having a negative effect on time.

We took a last stroll around the neighboring park, and I kept seeing myself in the race, flying along the route, more than ready to run. I couldn't help bouncing around when we joined the other runners for the start of the race. I had put in the work and felt confident I would reach my time goal, but reaching the finish line with a smile was the primary goal of my first marathon.

When the gun sounded, I was all smiles. At the half marathon mark at Vevey, my time was 1:33:56, a considerable cushion for my goal of 3 hours and 30 minutes. After the turning point at La Tour-de-Peilz, I knew I was doing well, but in the back of my mind, I knew that I might have to pay a price for flying too quickly through the first half. On the way back to Lausanne and the finish at Olympic Museum, I could almost taste the wine as I passed Rivaz, and though there were not many onlookers, their passionate cheers exhilarated me.

After about 2 hours and 37 minutes at approximately kilometer 35, the legendary Herr Hammermann struck. I was expecting him, but I wasn't expecting such vengeance. When my body made the fuel switch from carbohydrates to predominantly fat, I had to bite my teeth. Really. I bit my teeth so hard that I'm sure that I almost broke a filling. Herr Hammermann, or hitting the wall, was extreme because it was the first time my body had ever run out of carbohydrate reserves. It was unfamiliar territory for me. I had the feeling of not being able to put one foot in front of the other. I had to slow down for a while and may have let out a few grimaces, expletives, but I also yelled encouraging words to myself, and I eventually left Herr Hammermann behind after a few minutes and found my stride once again. What had helped me the most was visualizing the finish line. As soon as the pain had passed, I knew that nothing could stop me from finishing save a serious injury.

I crossed the finish line below the Olympic Museum with a time of 3:12:09. I could now say I had run a marathon! My time surpassed all my expectations, and I was proud of myself for accomplishing what I had set out to do. The joy I felt was not because of the time but rather the whole process. Shortly after finishing, I knew that it would not be my last marathon. And I also knew that this was the start of a journey, but I could not imagine at the time where that journey would lead me. I only knew that it had begun.

We are all visitors to this time, this place. We are just passing through. Our purpose here is to observe, to learn, to grow, to love, and then we return home.

Australian Aborigine proverb

A PERSON'S CURRENCY

Strip away the things a person has, the ornaments decorating the body and home, the brash and gaudy baubles, others simple, others perhaps even refined, and what do you have left?

The person is what is left, a person made up of actions and inactions, dreams and thoughts, fears, desires, love given, accepted, rebuked.

I have spent a great deal of time considering values on my runs, what I see as beautiful, what I admire, what I could share and give. Running through the forest near my home in the suburbs of Basel in the early morning, with the sky just catching light and the world waking to a new day, body gliding over soft earth surrounded by trees that came before me and will be standing long after I am gone, the cool air flowing over me, and there is birdsong, or it is my elation transmuting what I feel inside, and why am I here?

What is a man's currency? A person's currency, my currency? It's not the job I have, my position in a company, the money I have, my possessions, because you can take all those away from me. What you can't take away are what I have done, my knowledge and skills, and more than anything, what I have given and shared from my life, the knowledge and skills that I've accumulated. That is my currency and that's a person's currency. And the more you spend, the more currency you have.

What is my currency? The answer to this basic question is the heart of this book. Running has been my passion for

20 years, and the school of running has given me more currency than I would have ever imagined.

What amazes me is that the more you put into whatever your passion is or what brings you joy, what you receive grows exponentially because all the aspects, both little and large, that you work on improving, when you add them all together, the sum is so much bigger than the parts. Though I have yet to figure out the rate of interest, the sum grows and compounds year after year. I like to think of it as a jigsaw puzzle. One piece may seem insignificant on its own, but joined with the others, it completes a picture, and that picture becomes ever fuller: it is the picture of who I am.

I want to give more to others – and I'm not talking about money, as you know. Much of this book is about making a plan, training, discipline, "tuning out," advice on the Marathon des Sables.

More than anything, though, it is a journey of passion and joy, and if a person is lucky enough to have both of those, the pursuit of a passion pays dividends like nothing else in this world. And those dividends are to share.

STAGE ONE

TO THE BIVOUAC

"It's beyond your imagination," my coach had said from the beginning, and so far, the Marathon des Sables has bested all my mind had conjured as I cross an *oued* with another line of dunes that should lead to a plateau. I've covered nearly 18 kilometers and feel as if I'm more floating over the ground, a butterfly, than clomping along like a camel or the simple biped that I am – only 12 kilometers to go!

I had needed close to 1 hour and 23 minutes to reach the first checkpoint at kilometer 13, where I had refilled my water bottles. Though the sun has moved higher and is getting stronger, my body seems to be gaining strength with it or from it. I will soon start taking sips of water every 5 minutes, for one piece of advice, or rather commandment, that my coach always repeated was, "Thou shall be disciplined with water."

Timon Abegglen is my coach. Straight after signing up for the Marathon des Sables, I got in contact with Timon and asked him if he could help get me ready for the race. He's a two-time finisher, but this race even got the best of him one time, and he was forced to pull out due to foot problems. In case of foot swelling, which was Timon's problem, my shoes are a size and a half bigger than what I normally wear, and I'm wearing two pairs of socks for extra protection – a pair of marathon socks over toe socks. In case of swelling, I could get rid of one pair of socks to reduce volume. My feet feel fine up to now, but I know they will be at the front of the line in the back of my mind throughout the race, joined by water and what I'm carrying on my back. My backpack, snug and stable, is an extension of my body; it comforts, acts as a protective shell of sorts, and is nearly my entire home and sustenance while in the desert.

My internal checklist is all green checks that I can almost hear dinging in my head as I go through the list item by item. Networking is also on the list because you never know when you'll need assistance or can help your fellow runners – they are also there to share difficulties and triumphs. It's also good to speak to those who've done this before because it's often an accumulation of little things, tips and nuggets of wisdom, that can make a big difference when it comes to running and finishing an endurance race, especially one in the Sahara – bigger shoes, for example.

I'm floating; I'm in the run. I know my pace is probably too fast, but it feels right. My body tells me the pace it's moving at is what it wants. The dunes end, and there's a small hill to my left. I know from my map that around the hill is the next checkpoint, the second and final one before the finish.

I arrive at the checkpoint with a few other runners with a smile that is probably on the verge of being grotesque because it's so big, but I receive smiles in return from the others. I like to believe that smiles are more contagious than yawns. I've covered the 22.9 kilometers in a little over 2 hours and 36 minutes. As I fill my water bottles, I'm chattering away to everyone, to no one in particular, to myself. A fellow runner laughs with me, at me, and we give each other a brotherly handclasp and exchange nods that say good luck and a strong finish to you.

I'm in the dream that I've held for so long, and I am a part of what I had spent so many months training for and planning, and yes, it is beyond my imagination. It is real, it is all around me, and I charge off down the *oued*, the dried riverbed, with plenty of bounce in my legs.

I have less than 7 kilometers to go, but high noon is near, and its approach is first sensed by my mouth. I take a sip of water and give it swirl. I'll be taking a sip of water every 5 minutes now, not only to keep my body hydrated but also to keep my mouth and lips from gumming up. Anyone who has run in blistering heat – and for a man from Switzerland, temperatures around 40 degrees Celsius are blistering – knows that all the moisture in the mouth can be cooked out in only a few minutes, leaving the mouth full of sticky cotton. I've had some runs in high temperatures where it felt like I could peel off my lips and stick them on any surface, even Teflon, and you'd have trouble trying to scrape them off. I'm going to try to avoid that discomfort and just concentrate on floating through the last set of dunes in this first stage.

Floating? Why not flying! The dunes are unbelievably beautiful and give me a sense of freedom, and even better, they offer me freedom: they invite me to chart my own path over them. Though it may sound counterintuitive, you should avoid following in the footsteps of previous runners because the depth of each step is increased, which demands even more from you, and the sand is demanding enough as it is. Burning calves are inevitable going through the dunes because the surface gives, making it harder to plant the foot and requiring more energy to lift off than on firm surfaces. Having learned not to follow in a runner's footsteps from my coach helped, but my calves still start burning after a few hundred meters. And with the rising temperature, more air penetrates the sand, so my feet sink deeper, meaning the dunes will only get more difficult for me, but burning calves are a small price to pay for being where I am.

I see my path through the sand, the line I'll take, reading the dune for the firmest sand. Finding the best line is a real advantage, and I believe I have a knack for it. It helps knowing how dunes are formed. Sand builds up around an obstacle, such as a rock or a small clump of vegetation or even an animal carcass, and the wind flows around the obstacle and deposits sand on the leeward side of the obstacle, and it grows from there, with some dunes growing more than 300 meters. From what I've gathered, the highest dunes I will encounter in the race will be in the 150-meter range, expected on the very last day of the race. Dunes are a wonderful study of the power of patience and persistence. My path goes over the side of the dunes where the wind climbs over it and where it strikes it with the most force.

It's a lovely feeling reading the dunes. I feel like an explorer, and I could do it much longer, but after a kilometer and a half, the dunes give way to a sandy gorge, and then I move on to a stony valley. I only have a few kilometers to go, and my pace is still much faster than I had planned. I'm covered in sweat but my engine is firing on all cylinders. I can't believe that I'm about to finish the first stage of this race. I've been steadfast in sipping my water every 5 minutes even when joy was surging through me as I took in what was around me, and I kept asking myself, "Can you believe this? Can you believe you're here?"

There it is! I see the bivouac as I go through some small dunes, and this has to be one of the greatest finishing lines I've ever seen. I cross the finish with an official time of 3:40:05, 170th overall. I know my coach Timon would scold me for running much too fast, but as I cross the finish line, I raise my arms in the air in praise of being a part of this.

I feel humbled by beauty.

I want to hear a song by the ukulele player.

EMERGENCE OF AN IDEA

I likely heard about the Marathon des Sables shortly after it first took place in 1986. Back then, only 23 participants had dared to race over the relatively unknown terrain. I could hardly imagine that 31 years later, I would be one of almost 1,200 participants at the starting line. I would have had too much respect for such an inhuman challenge in the Sahara. Right from the beginning, though, pictures and reports on the Marathon des Sables fascinated me, again and again. Somehow, my beloved wife, Monika, must have noticed.

In early July 2016, Monika and I were sitting on the terrace of our holiday apartment in Grindelwald. It's our little jewel that has a view of the 3,970-meter Eiger. It was a warm summer day, and as we sometimes do, we were waiting to see the first mountaineers climbing the majestic and world-renowned north face, weather permitting. With my Zeiss telescope, which I received as a gift from the guests at my 50th birthday party, I was scanning the mountain.

I had recovered from the ruptured tendon at the back of my left thigh, probably suffered while skiing the winter before – it was a rather unnecessary tribute to carving! Wanting to be on the safe side, I had signed up for the 51-kilometer distance at that year's Eiger Ultra Trail: 101 kilometers would probably be too far just coming out of several months of rehab. There was something else bothering me, however. I couldn't stop thinking about it. How long could I expect my body to cover distances of more than a hundred kilometers in mountain terrain? I shared that concern with Monika while we sat on the terrace, the sun already heating up the morning air.

My ultimate wish, I told her, was to enrich my running career with at least one more emotional highlight, perhaps as early as next year. It could even be the end of my running of ultras.

At that time, I had no idea what ultra it would be, but this did not seem to have been the case for Monika. Suddenly, and without hesitation, she said that from her point of view, there was only one option. "The Marathon des Sables in the Moroccan Sahara. You have been carrying it around for so long, and now is the time for you to sign up for it," she said.

"What!" I was quite surprised by her words. At first, it was I who was a bit skeptical. "Are you sure I could get through it?" I asked.

"You definitely can," she said, referring again and again to my excellent physical condition and mental toughness. "You have never been more ready, especially in your head, than you are right now."

Many of the articles I had read about the Marathon des Sables had highlighted mental strength as an essential prerequisite for finishing. They also said that the preparation for the one-week desert adventure meant a lot of time and commitment, which meant compromises when it came to family life. That was the first thing I said to Monika. "That's ok," she said, "from now on, I'll be part of the project."

I am infinitely grateful to her for that. For me, that was a precondition in taking the idea to the next level. The fact that my wife was "sending me into the desert," so to speak, got big laughs from the people I shared my plan with, and it was a running gag at various keynotes that I gave after my return from the desert.

I also had to convince our two daughters, Manuela and Simone, of the feasibility of the upcoming adventure, and Monika also helped me with that. Admittedly, it was anything but easy. I can understand that it can be beyond the imagination of non-runners that someone would willingly cover about 250 kilometers in seven days in the heat of the Sahara equipped with only the bare necessities. And in my case, I would be doing it at the not really young age of 57.

Even though I was well aware and had to learn to accept that performance would decline every year without mercy, I did not consider age to be a real risk factor. Years of experience correlated with my mental strength, and so, in a way, it compensated for my getting older. In addition, I was sure that I knew my body well enough from all the years of long-distance running. I have learned to listen to even the slightest signals of my body and to take them seriously. I have also developed confidence over the years, and that would help me overcome any small crises in a long-distance competition. It is the recurring highs and lows that make ultrarunners resistant to and capable of suffering.

"Did not finish," or DNF as the initialism it is commonly known as, was out of the question for me, but I promised my daughters that I would stop the race should any medical issues arise. Manuela and Simone always demand absolute promises from me, and so I took my vows.

Now nothing stood in the way of me registering for the Marathon des Sables 2017. I went to the organizer's website and carefully read through everything that was of interest and importance to me. I quickly accessed the information about what to do to secure a starting place at the coveted event, and I completed my registration on the morning of July 5, 2016. Immediately after, I made the first deposit.

There is a significant price tag attached to the Marathon des Sables, but in return, I got something very special and unique. It was worth every euro.

I forwent the option of taking a charter flight from Paris, preferring to fly to Marrakesh from my hometown of Basel. Marco Jaeggi, a Swiss running colleague of mine, from whom I would get many valuable tips in the coming weeks, had done the same the year before, and he recommended it to me.

After registering, I spent the first few weeks working on the structure of the preparation phase. Compared to previous races, there was a lot more preparation to do than simply the physical part.

WEST AGUENOUN N'OUMERHIOUT
to
RICH MBIRIKA

STAGE TWO

STRING OF PEARLS

El Otfal.

Right after we were handed the roadbook on the bus ride from Ouarzazate to the desert, it was clear that the second day would give us one of the most impressive moments of the race: Jebel El Otfal, the famed mountain with an unbelievably steep and exhausting ascent and an equally steep descent on the back through deep sand and boulders. My Swiss colleague and tentmate Markus Stöcklin had almost prayed at the hotel in Ouarzazate – where we had spent three nights together before the race – that we would climb Jebel El Otfal, and what a loud cheer he let out on the bus when he opened the roadbook. We would even pass the mountain again on the third day from the other side. The organizers made a bonus for us runners when they mapped the course.

We had set out from the bivouac at 8:30 in the morning, and I reached the first checkpoint at kilometer 12.8 in 1 hour and 28 minutes (I'm not superstitious, but 12.8 and 1:28 mean something positive to someone, I would hope, and hope is powerful).

It's 10 in the morning, and the sky is almost lapis lazuli, a deep blue that tells us that the sun will show no mercy today. We are now like a string of pearls stretching over several kilometers, and long stretches of sand await, challenging terrain that will alternate between small dunes and sandy hills. Only about 20%

of the Sahara is covered with sand. The vast majority of the desert is stony and rocky, called *hammada*, and the gravel part of the desert is known as *serir*. The Sahara is nearly as big as the continental United States and is the largest desert in the world. It is seven and a half times bigger than the Gobi Desert, which is the second largest. The Arabs also call the Sahara *bhar bila ma*, which roughly translates to "sea without water."

Only trudging over hard ground and stubbing our toes on rocks wouldn't be as romantic, would it? It would not be the Marathon des Sables, the epic race through the desert sands that most people picture in their minds. The organizers made sure that the course crosses long stretches of sand to fit the picture that most of us have of the desert. As for sand, a grain weighs approximately 200 micrograms, which is around fifty times the weight of an ovum, a human egg cell. To reach the weight of the Eiffel Tower, you need 36.5 trillion grains of sand. Large numbers have always impressed me, a fact that seems to be rooted in my attraction to mathematics.

I arrive at Checkpoint 2 after 3 hours and 12 minutes. I have covered 25.5 kilometers, and the heat is already beating down ruthlessly with another 13.5 kilometers to go, including the steep climb and descent of El Otfal. I line up for water – everything is very well organized, with lanes divided by bib numbers. It is always the same ritual: getting my water card punched, taking the ration of 1.5 or 3 liters of water, and then the desperate hunt for some shade by one of the escort vehicles. The water card is important: you must always have it with you and have it punched at each and every checkpoint. Missing punch holes in your water card are not only sanctioned with time penalties, but if you miss too many, you get disqualified. There is zero tolerance when it comes to safety, and that is a good thing. Everyone who has felt the heat of the desert would agree.

I have a short break of a few minutes at each checkpoint, and the plan going into the race was to eat at a middle checkpoint during a long stage, like today. It turned out to be a smart decision. After I find my shady spot at the side of an off-road vehicle, I lean against the side door, relax my mind, and prepare to feed my body the fuel it will need to see me over and down the mountain.

I am prepared. I am a planner. I have Peronin and Datrex bars, and I had repeatedly tested each in conditions that were as close as possible to what I believed were racing conditions. As I usually do, I had minimized as many risks as I possibly could.

Peronin is a meal replacement developed for endurance athletes, and with 448 kilocalories per 100 grams of powder, it is a real energy bomb (one kilocalorie equals the amount of energy needed to heat one kilogram of water by one degree Celsius).

I opted for Peronin with cocoa flavor, as I admit to having a sweet tooth on occasion. I am Swiss. Chocolate. It makes sense, doesn't it?

You dissolve the powder in water and drink it. Child's play.

Well, sometimes things turn out a little differently than planned. During my intensive training phase, I had stopped during my long runs and mixed a bottle of Peronin, and it had worked great, really giving me an extra kick for the last part of my runs. The training phase was in winter, though, and that is where I had miscalculated. Drinking Peronin with cold water is fine, but I am choking and gagging with every swallow at the side of the vehicle. I raise my hand to let some runners know that I am okay. Peronin is not the same when the water is 35 degrees Celsius. I eventually get it down because I have to. These extra calories are going to be essential.

Next up is one of the two Datrex bars I took with me. Developed for the United States Coast Guard, Datrex is a true high-tech food packed with energy. The bars immediately crumble as I try to remove them from the wrapper, and if that is not challenging enough, the dusty bits that I put in my mouth suck out all the moisture. It is almost like chewing on paste, like putting flour in your mouth. I get the bars down, but this little pit stop has not gone as I had imagined it would, but such is an ultra. No matter how well prepared you believe you are, the unexpected happens. I have to laugh. It has been a miserable pit stop, but my body feels good and has the energy it needs. You live, and you learn, and that is what racing and life are about; celebration too, because if everything in life always fell into place with certainty, and our journey mapped and marked to the finest detail, why would we ever feel like dancing? There wouldn't be space for joy.

Before leaving my spot of shade, I take a quick look at the roadbook to get an idea of the expected terrain. I rise from the ground, shake my legs out, and head out toward the mountain.

Shortly before Jebel El Otfal, Ricarda and Jens Witzel join me, two of my five tentmates and a long-time couple. They both have already completed an incredible number of ultras, numbering over 100, including the 135-mile Badwater Ultramarathon in 2017 that they ran together in California's Death Valley, the hottest place on earth. I got to know Ricarda while running my second Swissalpine Marathon in 2006 when we ran together for the last 15 kilometers through the beautiful Dischma, the alpine valley southeast from Davos, to the finish. When I heard that Ricarda had also signed up for the Marathon des Sables 2017, a circle seemed to close.

One thing that makes the Marathon des Sables special is the sometimes clear view of the upcoming route. And today, it is pronounced: the peak of Jebel El Otfal looms before me.

I reach the summit of the Jebel El Otfal at around kilometer 34, and the beauty of the panorama leaves me nearly breathless. The climb was challenging, but I had no problems getting up it. I am more worried about getting down.

I'm enjoying standing on top of Jebel El Otfal, an approximately 15-kilometer long range of hills and the continuation of Jebel Maharch. I have been on much higher peaks in my life – not surprising for a person born in Switzerland – but the view from up here is undoubtedly one of the most beautiful I have ever had. You can smell the desert, and the light breeze is very welcome. Far off, the horizon blurs and flickers, and this flickering occurs when rays of light are bent when passing through air layers of different temperatures.

As I remember from school, the flickering is known as a Fata Morgana and may result in seeing an oasis when there is, in fact, not one. The name Fata Morgana is rooted in Italian and attributed to a fairy figure from the Arthurian legend. Morgana lived on the island of Avalon, which was inaccessible to mortals. When Italians "discovered" a non-existent island in the Strait of Messina, they associated it with Avalon and called the phenomenon Fata Morgana.

The roadbook warns of the high technical demands of the descent from Jebel El Otfal, which at times has a gradient of more than 20 percent. I begin descending on sand, and the feeling of flying almost elicits a veritable primal scream. The following stony passages require my utmost attention, for the danger of tumbling down is real, and I want to avoid that. For the first time, the hours of foot exercises that were part of my training should pay off. My coach, Timon, had put together a very efficient exercise program that I had strictly followed – I did specific foot exercises once or twice a week. The increased flexibility of the tendons and ligaments in my feet is a blessing, and they readily absorb a slight buckling or twist.

Finishing the descent, I already have the bivouac in my sights. It is only a few kilometers off, but it is noon now, and the heat has climbed and is cooking our bodies. I am making sure to drink some water every 5 minutes. I am applying the highest discipline to drinking.

At kilometer 35.6, I reach the last checkpoint at just under 5 hours and 34 minutes. I make a short break after receiving my water ration and then move on to tackle the finish at kilometer 39.

It is a real increase in distance from the first day's 30.3 kilometers. I feel exhausted, and that's due to going over Jebel El Otfal. With heavy legs, I wonder if maybe I have started the race a bit too fast. But then I say to myself, "Well, even if I have been too fast, there's no way to change it now," and I try to free myself from negative thoughts as quickly as I can. I will need to keep a positive head if I am going to get through the week, and being positive is what I consider one of my greatest strengths. You learn to be positive as an ultrarunner because if you are not positive, it would be impossible to finish such a race.

I cross the finish line with a time of 6:04:21, and my reward is a cup of Moroccan mint tea, a green tea with lots of spearmint. The Moroccan national drink, with its fresh mint aroma, waits for us at the finish of the stages and is a wonderful sign that my desert experience is one day richer. I have now covered a quarter of the total distance of the Marathon des Sables. As I sip my tea, I reflect on being in the middle of a goal that has been in my sights for a long time. I am in the midst of a dream that I have made real, and I do not want it to stop. I am within this moment in the desert, a moment that reaches out to the future and my past.

I am overwhelmed with emotions as I make my way to tent number 35, the home I am sharing throughout the week with five other Swiss runners.

PREPARATION AND EQUIPMENT

Since the majority of work in my profession of consulting is project related, it was natural for me to see the Marathon des Sables as a project.

To help me with my physical preparation, I engaged Timon Abegglen, a multiple finisher of the Marathon des Sables and an experienced coach. The structured and well-balanced training program started in mid-November 2016, kicking off with a partial circumnavigation of Lake Neuchâtel. Those 49 kilometers were also the ultimate test of whether or not my ruptured hamstring tendon had fully recovered, and it passed the test without a hint of soreness. In the weeks and months after, I tried to stick as close as possible to the plan Timon created for me. The plan called for me to run approximately 1,400 kilometers in 150 hours, and also included bodyweight training, TRX, foot exercises, and cross-training on my stationary bike.

In the first phase of my preparation between July and October 2016, I also set out to find out as much as possible through discussions with previous participants of the Marathon des Sables. I was impressed from the very beginning by the openness of everyone and their willingness to share knowledge and experiences. I learned a great deal regarding equipment and nutrition from the numerous conversations I had, and I also did a lot of research on the internet and went through many blog posts. Starting my preparation early also gave me the possibility to try out variations in my training, though, of course, one cannot really create desert-like conditions in Switzerland.

Marco Jaeggi, who completed the Marathon des Sables in 2016, was the first person I spoke with about the race. He and I talked about it over lunch in a Thai takeaway restaurant in Jegensdorf in the Canton of Bern. Birgit Steiger and Markus Stöcklin – who both became tentmates during my participation in 2017 – my coach Timon Abegglen, Brigitte Daxelhoffer and also Anke Molkenthin, who won the Marathon des Sables in 1996, all helped me a lot and allowed me to look at my upcoming adventure from different perspectives and angles. The most important thing, however, was that all these conversations assured me that I would focus on the right things, the essential things, and that was very important for me. I wanted to eliminate as many risks as possible that could have arisen because of poor preparation.

In the autumn, I slowly narrowed down my equipment and nutrition choices – I was determined to make a final selection by the end of January 2017 at the latest. I wanted to focus on my physical preparation for the final stretch, as well as the many small things that I would still need to do.

Several previous finishers of the Marathon des Sables had told me that if I managed not to have any significant problems with my feet, I would already have won half the battle of finishing. I decided on the shoe model early on: it was the Brooks Cascadia, the shoe in which I have completed the most ultra runs and in which I feel most comfortable.

The real *pièce de résistance*, so to speak, was choosing the right shoe size. One of the biggest unknowns during a multi-day race in the desert is how the feet will react to the strain of being in extreme conditions. One can and should assume that foot volume increases with activity, and getting a larger-than-normal shoe size even for normal conditions is advisable. And for extreme conditions? But how much bigger? The experiences of previous participants were so different that, in the end, I had to decide on my own strategy. I went the extra mile and tried out three different sizes in long and extensive training sessions: one, one-and-a-half, and two sizes above my normal size of 44.5 for that shoe model. As mentioned earlier, my choice, in the end, was my normal size plus one-and-a-half, a size 46, with two layers of socks. That gave me the possibility to get rid of one layer in case of swelling of the feet.

Then there were the gaiters, and here I chose the model of a well-known French manufacturer. A valuable tip from Timon came into play here. The gaiters come with Velcro straps for attaching them to the shoes, but Timon urged me to have the Velcro straps glued and sewn on to the shoes by a professional shoemaker. He suggested a shoemaker located at Fabrikstrasse close to my office in Zurich.

The shoemaker, Antonio, has been attaching gaiters for Swiss Marathon des Sables participants for years. Timon asked me to please send kind greetings to Antonio and assured me that I would be very satisfied with Antonio's work. And so I was. The Velcro straps were perfectly mounted, and not even a small part of the permeable mesh was visible. Sand relentlessly finds its way through the smallest openings, and to me, it was a strategy of avoidance that would pay off, and it sure did. I was almost able to count with my ten fingers the grains of sand that found their way into my shoes during the Marathon des Sables.

The evaluation of clothing was a constant back and forth. My original long list became a short list, and though weight played a role in my final choice, comfort was also a factor. For the clothes I planned to wear during the day, comfort and familiarity were the decisive selection criteria. In the end, I chose the Salomon running shorts that I was familiar with, the ones with light compression inners to help blood circulation.

The Marathon des Sables follows the principle of self-sufficiency. During the race, only water is available at the various checkpoints and at the bivouacs where the stages finish. Everything else, the clothing, the mandatory equipment, the marathon kit handed over by the organizers, food and any other personal belongings, is carried in the backpack by the athletes throughout the week, and the weight of the backpack must be between 6.5 and 15.0 kilograms when checking in at the first bivouac. This target weight does not include any water. The organizers meticulously observe the rules and regulations throughout the entire competition. The safety of the participants is paramount, and the extreme conditions in the desert do not allow for even the smallest avoidable risk.

Packing was a bigger challenge than I thought it was going to be. I repeatedly packed and unpacked my backpack at home, starting anew each time to get it right. In the beginning, it was a mystery to me how all the individual items spread out on the floor in front of me could possibly fit in the rather small looking backpack.

During my preparation time and in the desert itself, I found some real pack optimizers. "Every gram counts" is the axiom to follow, and that means the complete removal of all superfluous attachments on and inside the backpack, which includes the shortening of carrying straps and the removal of inner pockets. I didn't dare shorten all the straps as a first-time participant, as I was scared I would end up cutting away a little too much. But I saw that some people had even drilled holes in the shaft of their toothbrush to save 1 to 2 grams of weight. Some also made their own slippers to cut weight, while I relied on a somewhat weight-optimized minimalist huarache style slipper that I found on the internet. My tentmate Markus Stöcklin was one of those packing champions. He helped me a lot during my preparation time and also during the days before the start at the hotel we were staying at in Ouarzazate, where he gave me valuable last-minute advice. Markus's backpack weighed just 6.5 kilograms at the check-in at the first bivouac, which is precisely the minimum. The fact that he only managed to reach the minimum weight by adding a couple of oranges for his first breakfast was a testament to his experience and sophisticated packing tactics. His two previous participations in the Marathon des Sables had obviously paid off.

My backpack ended up weighing 7.3 kilograms, which was quite good for a first-time participant, or at least that was the feedback I received from more experienced desert runners. Looking back, I'm pretty sure I could have saved at least another

500 grams. I simply played it extra safe here and there, which was probably unnecessary, looking back on it.

Selecting hygiene supplies was difficult at first. I even carefully counted the toilet paper: exactly six sheets per day was what I decided on based on various feedback and tips. When I asked an experienced Marathon des Sables participant what I should do if I developed a bowel problem, he laconically said that then even 100 sheets would not be enough. Ok, I thought, and though I took note of his non-motivational interjection, I stuck to my plan of six sheets per day – I used the last sheet at 5:30 a.m. on the last day before the start of the concluding Charity Stage.

For my personal hygiene, I also afforded myself the luxury of some chamomile-scented wet wipes, which added 37 grams of extra weight. Admittedly, a pure luxury, but that subtle scent of chamomile gave me the feeling that I actually had undergone a thorough body cleansing. Tooth tabs, toothpicks, and a toothbrush finally completed my personal hygiene set, all somewhat weight-optimized.

In the end, my packing list contained more than 70 individual items, including everything I would be carrying on my body during the stages, with the latter coming in at just over 1.8 kilograms.

Since my participation, I have already happily advised several Marathon des Sables rookies on preparation and selecting gear and nutrition. One of the great things in ultrarunning is the spirit between runners, which is very much about giving and taking advice.

RICH MBIRIKA
to
NORTH EL MAHARCH

STAGE THREE

CALL OF THE BERBERS

"*Yalla*! *Yalla*!"

Yalla resounds through the bivouac as it does every morning, the unmistakable sign that we will soon be sitting around on the Berber carpet without a roof over our heads. The carpet gives at least some protection from the partly stony ground – and some stones are sharp.

The Berbers call out, "*Yalla*! *Yalla*!" as they effortlessly dismantle the tents in a few steps, skillfully fold the blankets, and then load them onto the trucks for transport to the next bivouac. In English, *yalla* means come on, let's go, hurry up. And these men always seem to be in a good mood.

I am the tentmate who has everything already neatly stowed in his backpack as two Berbers remove our roof. My status is race-pack-ready. Getting my pack together early on gives me structure, which is a kind of comfort at the beginning of the day and allows me to concentrate on my mental preparation for the upcoming challenge under the desert sun.

I have already eaten breakfast, having mixed my daily porridge shortly after waking up around 5:30 in the morning. I chose porridge with blueberries from a maker of high-tech food. One portion of the freeze-dried meal contains 452 kcal. It is an excellent nutrient boost. I mixed it with 250 milliliters of cold water. Re-hydration takes about 15 minutes. Unfortunately, the sweet taste of the dish, which was tasty on the first two mornings, had become so repugnant to me that I had to force myself to swallow it down spoonful by spoonful. Some calories didn't make it as I couldn't eat the whole portion even though I knew I should. One important lesson learned is that I should switch to a salty breakfast after a couple of days if I ever enter such an adventurous race again. I know what I would pack next time: scrambled eggs with peppers and tomatoes enriched with oven-dried bacon.

Like every day, we'll now spend a good hour under the open sky and literally absorb the first rays of sunlight. Each morning I enjoy feeling the first sunbeams warming up my body. It was relatively cool again during the night – I would estimate a low of about 5 degrees Celsius – and bathing in the rising sun is a warm welcome. As the sun rises, an almost meditative atmosphere develops with the spreading light. All the tents have been dismantled and the carpets rolled up and turned into improvised seating, which almost everybody uses. Why waste unnecessary energy walking or standing around if there is another way to bridge the time until the start of the race?

At 8:00 a.m., we are asked to move to the starting area. "*Yalla!*" Looking at the crowd of runners moving towards the start corridor gives me goosebumps. If you could capture this moment in a motif and put it in paint on a wall or trap it in wallpaper, you'd have the compressed nervous energy of all the runners visualizing what lies ahead. I am unsure what kind of effect it would have on a room, but I am sure the room would be blasting rock and roll even when silent. It is the same at the start of every race I have ever run.

Our tent group gathers at the starting line as we always do. We psyche each other up one last time and wish one another a successful day. I give my race pack a last check; everything seems to be properly lashed and stashed, and I have two filled bottles on the front belt and one 1.5-liter PET bottle fixed in the loops on top of my front pack.

I can hear the music that has become one of the hymns of this week for me: America's "A Horse with No Name."

"After two days in the desert sun..."

The song, its tone and structure, always reminds me of one of my favorite singers and songwriters, Neil Young.

"After three days in the desert fun
I was looking at a riverbed..."

What a song!

It is the same ritual every morning. Patrick Bauer stands on the roof of an off-road vehicle – there are 120 in the convoy that moves with us through the desert. Patrick, assisted by a female translator, gives us the last instructions for the stage ahead. He obviously enjoys this role, and his energy and enthusiasm is the ultimate evidence of how much he is part of the Marathon des Sables. In 1986, he welcomed 23 runners who embarked on a week-long adventure in the Moroccan Sahara at the first Marathon des Sables. That was the birth of an incredible success story. This is the 32nd event, and there are almost 1,200 athletes at the starting line.

Shortly before the start, the Marathon des Sables anthem echoes through the desert at full volume. Patrick sends us on our journey with "Highway to Hell" by AC/DC, and I've still got my goosebumps, and that is hard to beat.

On the first hilltop at about kilometer 2.5, I'm once more overwhelmed by the desert landscape and its sharp color contrasts in the early morning. I feel like a tiny part of a great spectacle. The play of changing colors during the day sometimes looks unreal.

Slowly but steadily, my backpack is getting a little lighter each day. It may sound like a small detail, but it's not: I have unburdened myself by about 1.2 kilos in total, and I try to imagine each step becoming easier. Each daypack weighs on average 550 grams – the meals for one day. I had carefully prepared all of them at home, reducing each pack's size as much as possible by using a vacuum sealer I purchased specifically for that purpose.

After about 8 kilometers, I find myself atop Jebel Joua Baba Ali. According to the roadbook, there is a rather technical passage on the ridge in front of me. As an experienced mountain runner, I'm fairly used to this kind of terrain and know I will have fun on this part of the stage. I witness some fellow runners falling down, but nothing too bad as far as I can tell. Fortunately, I have been spared from such misfortunes so far.

After a rather demanding descent that also crossed a dune, I soon reach the first checkpoint. I head to the lane marked 370-569: my bib number is 455. As I enter it to get to the water delivery point, I quickly take a few sips of my nearly empty bottle and pour the remaining few drops over my head. It feels really good!

"Are you ok? Did you take your salt?" I immediately answer, "Yes! Yes!" like two shots from a gun. I do not want to raise any doubts due to an unnecessarily delayed response. I get my PET bottle with 1.5 liters of fresh water marked with my bib number to prevent any possible confusion and to identify the owner should a bottle be disposed of at an unauthorized place. To be sanctioned with a time penalty due to the improper disposal of a bottle would probably fall into the category of human stupidity.

The sun is already beating down mercilessly, and I take the opportunity to stand in the shade of one of the off-road vehicles for some minutes. I open a fresh bottle of water, swallow two salt tablets, and shortly after I make off towards Checkpoint 2. My watch shows 1 hour and 25 minutes since the start.

After about 2 kilometers I have left a rather steep ascent with an estimated gradient of 15%. A 15% ascent means that after 100 meters, I will have climbed approximately 15 meters – the tangent of the angle times 100 as we all learned in school. This is followed by a passage on the ridge of almost 2 kilometers.

Suddenly, on the ridge, I spot a black bird circling above me. I did not expect to see a bird here. It is a desert raven with a considerable wingspan, and I watch it for a long time. I learn later that the *Corvus rificollis* likes to build its nests on rock faces, and there are quite a few of these in this part of the Sahara.

The graceful movement of the bird's wings reminds me of an earlier time when my life was supposed to follow a different path and, unexpectedly, a happy coincidence took it in another direction. Sometimes I wonder why life takes a particular course at a specific moment, and in such moments I tend to believe in predetermination.

As a young boy, my great dream was to become a professional pilot. This wish had taken hold of me early in my teens, following other ones in early childhood, like becoming an Alpine herdsman. I started learning how to fly at that tender age of 16 and got my pilot's license before I had even driven a car. I was particularly proud of my aerobatics rating, which I obtained a few years later. I still remember my flights with the legendary Bücker Jungmann very well. The only testimonies of me flying that plane are some yellowed photos – digital photography started long afterward. We even had to use jumper cables connected to my Mini Cooper to start the Bücker's engine. Funny stuff!

Unfortunately, I did not succeed in the final step in becoming a Swiss military pilot. And later it turned out that I suffered from a latent red-green visual impairment, which made it impossible to pursue the profession of pilot. A great dream had been destroyed, but I quickly found my way back to positive thinking, which is one of my strengths, even back then. I then decided to devote myself to the completion of my studies.

In 1984 I received my degree in actuarial mathematics at the University of Basel. Following my studies, I joined IBM's branch office, and this is the happy coincidence (destiny?) of my life story, where I met my beloved wife, Monika. We have been married for more than 33 years now and have two wonderful daughters, Manuela and Simone. So, in retrospect, everything took the path it had to take, and I ended up meeting my Monika at my first employer only because a big dream fell through. That big dream was replaced by an even bigger one!

The raven is drawing big circles in the sky.

After another very steep, sandy descent, I reach a wide valley that I'll cross for the next 5 kilometers. I feel like I'm in an oven now, and I know that this is one of those phases of the race when drinking discipline is a must. Shortly before the start of the ascent of Jebel El Otfal, this time from the other side, I arrive at Checkpoint 2 after a little more than 2 hours and 51 minutes. I collect my water, put high-tech powder into one of my water bottles, and drink it empty in more or less one go. At this checkpoint, I take a little more time than usual before setting off for the ascent of Jebel El Otfal, which is incredibly steep and on difficult ground.

On the ascent, the trail is secured on the last section by ropes, help that I gratefully accept. And suddenly I hear him again, the ukulele player, who, incredibly, catches me from behind. *"Aux Champs-Elysées, aux Champs-Elysées, au soleil, sous la pluie, à midi ou à minuit, il y a tout ce que vous voulez aux Champs-Elysées."* This wonderful and unforgettable song dedicated to the famous boulevard in Paris was originally released by the British psychedelic pop group Jason Crest under the name "Waterloo Road" and later interpreted by Joe Dassin in 1969. It is now with me for the next meters of the ascent. The ukulele reminds me of my time at secondary school. My singing teacher used to play it regularly. The ukulele usually employs four strings, with the top string set one octave higher, which gives the ukulele its unmistakable sound. I join in with the chorus *"Aux Champs-Elysées."*

Shortly after noon, I reach the apex of Jebel El Otfal; a little more than a half-marathon lies behind me now. The descent towards the bivouac leads me through a dried riverbed, an *oued*, in the Maghreb zone, and I can already see our bivouac for the upcoming night. But there are still about 10 kilometers to the finish, and it feels like I have to fight for every meter. The clear view speaks of vastness.

I leave the last 100 meters behind and reach the finish of the third stage. Another 31.6 kilometers have been covered today, and my watch shows 5:37:36. I wear my usual GPS watch, but I only use it as a conventional timepiece. The battery power would not suffice for the whole week with the GPS switched on, and carrying a power bank for recharging was not an option for me due to the substantial additional weight. Nevertheless, I wanted to have my familiar timepiece with me, which admittedly had more mental than practical reasons.

I arrive at our tent, number 35, and Jens, Ricarda, and Simon are already there – Simon Gruner is also a tentmate. To my delight, the floor under the Berber carpet has already been cleared of stones and branches, and after a few minutes, I say goodbye and fall into a short, deep sleep.

I feel like I earned it.

ARRIVAL IN MOROCCO

It was Monday, April 3, 2017. There were only six days to go before the start of the Marathon des Sables, and I was heading to Morocco. The first stop from Basel was Marrakesh, where I would spend a few days to acclimate myself and get into the right frame of mind for my forthcoming adventure in the desert.

The last training sessions in Switzerland had gone pretty well, and two long runs over the weekend at a rather slow pace starting from my home had given me the certainty that I had done enough training.

I had divided my luggage into two pieces: the backpack I would be carrying through the desert throughout the week, and a large duffel bag. I had chosen a striking yellow color for the duffel bag so that I could immediately recognize it, be it at the airport on the baggage carousel or in one of the depots in Morocco. In the backpack was all the equipment and food I would need while in the desert. The backpack was my carry-on luggage as I wanted to avoid the risk that my equipment and food, carefully evaluated and selected over months, would be left behind due to a handling problem at the airport. Since the transport of fuel tablets is not allowed in either hand or checked baggage, I would make use of the opportunity to obtain them at the first bivouac. That was a small but essential detail because getting stopped by airport security would be rather silly and unnecessary.

Unsure if I could pass security at Basel Airport with all my vacuumed food, some of it even in powder form, I had spoken with the border police at a previous arrival at the airport, and luckily, I had been told that all would be fine, but that I should be sure to take along all product declarations to have the necessary proof if needed, which I did.

On the flight to Morocco, I used the time to relax with music. I also took a book with me I had bought shortly before, *Wild by Nature*, by Sarah Marquis. The book recounts her adventure of walking from Siberia to Australia in 2010. This Swiss woman crossed the Gobi Desert, the jungle of Laos, and the Australian outback all on her own. I thought it was a perfect book to read to conclude my mental preparation for the Marathon des Sables.

The plan was to spend the first night in Morocco at Habib's home in Marrakesh. Habib Ait Ali had studied in Germany and has worked as a tourist guide in Morocco for many years. Monika and I got to know him on our trip to Marrakesh in October 2009, and since then, Habib has become a friend of our family. He also runs a bazaar in the middle of the Medina of Marrakesh. I was very much looking forward to my time with Habib, which was also an ideal opportunity to get in the right mood and adapt to the country and its people.

Habib picked me up at the airport shortly before 6:00 p.m. and drove us to his apartment in Gueliz, a "new town" of Marrakesh.

Habib showed me to my room for the night and then disappeared to the kitchen, where he started to prepare a Moroccan dinner for the two of us and whoever else might show up for a visit. The smells soon filled the apartment and made me look forward to what I knew was going to be a real feast. Habib is an excellent cook.

And it was a feast. There was grilled fish, a vegetable stew, and bread. Though I limited myself to the vegetarian part of the meal, that did not stop us from raising our glasses filled with an excellent local red wine and toasting our reunion. I declined the fish because I wanted to exclude the possibility of upsetting my stomach so shortly before the start of my desert adventure. I would not eat meat until after I had left the desert. Not eating meat was a small detail, but for me, those little details add up and increase my comfort level.

Habib and I told each other news about our families. We hadn't seen each other for a long time, too long in fact. He asked how Monika, Manuela, and Simone were doing. He lives part-time in Graz, where his wife grew up. "Right now, she is with the kids at the seaside in Essaouira," Habib said. "But when you return from the desert, they should all be here, and they are all looking forward to meeting you." It would be the first time I would meet Habib's family.

There was a coming and going of friends and relatives at Habib's home that evening. Hugs here, kisses there, and joy was everywhere. I was getting my fill of the local atmosphere! The hospitality in Morocco is hard to beat.

After breakfast the next morning, Habib drove us to the Medina quarter, the old part of the city. Habib and I had a few hours before the driver he had ordered for me would arrive. The driver would pick me up at his apartment in Gueliz and drive me from Marrakesh across the Atlas Mountains to Ouarzazate, a trip of about 4 hours.

From the parking lot at the entrance of the Medina, we walked through the Djemaa el-Fna, the central square in Marrakesh. Djemaa el-Fna has been on UNESCO's list of Masterpieces of the Oral and Intangible Heritage of Humanity since 2001. Unfortunately, there is also a dark side to the square. Sultans once used the square for executions and displayed impaled heads there. And in spring 2011, there was a terror attack in which 17 people died at the Café Argana, a well-known tourist spot.

I paused for a moment at the café and thought of the victims. Monika and I had sat at the square for hours in 2009 and were greatly impressed by the setting and unique ambiance. Towards evening, a colorful hustle and bustle starts on the Djemaa el-Fna. Musicians, snake charmers, jugglers, and other colorful characters create a feeling of wonder, and numerous street kitchens invite visitors to sample Moroccan street food.

At the only open stand so early in the morning, Habib and I drank freshly squeezed orange juice. We then walked through the narrow alleys in the souk to Habib's bazaar. What a jewel he had created! There were carpets and Moroccan handicrafts as far as the eye could see. We climbed up to the roof terrace where one of his employees had already started preparing a Moroccan tea for us with fresh Moroccan mint mixed with green tea and lots of sugar. I enjoyed the silence and smells of the souk in the early morning couldn't help thinking that life is damn beautiful in such moments.

The plan was for Habib to drive me back to his apartment after lunch to meet the driver. But after lunch, also taken on the terrace, Habib told me that a friend of his would give me a ride on his motorcycle back to Gueliz. Habib needed to stay in the bazaar to welcome customers who had announced they would be coming at short notice.

"Your friend is taking me on a motorcycle?" I couldn't help picturing scenes of Daniel Craig's wild ride as James Bond in Skyfall through the Grand Bazaar in Istanbul, but I tried to suppress my imagination as much as possible.

The ride on the motorcycle was almost as adventurous as I thought it would be. My knees barely missed sideswiping bazaar fronts and goods – by less than 5 centimeters at times – as we sped through the narrow streets of the medina. I have to admit that I was more than a little anxious. I felt like I was in an adventure before the real one had even begun. Pictures of shattered kneecaps raced by in my thoughts. Everything turned out well in the end, though, and Habib's friend dropped me off fully intact at the apartment.

The driver was already there waiting for me. I retrieved my backpack and duffel bag and climbed into the off-road vehicle. We were off to Ouarzazate.

The last suburbs of Marrakesh were soon behind us. I had read that the road over the Col du Tichka is one of the most beautiful passes in the world, and I was not disappointed. The summit is 2,260 meters above sea level, and the view on the drive up was indescribably beautiful. Oaks and olive trees lined the road built by French Foreign Legionnaires. The road passes small Berber villages, areas of rugged cliffs, with great views of gorges and valleys. From an altitude of about 1,800 meters, the roadside is marked by red and yellow-striped poles, an unmistakable indication that snow falls here in winter.

We took a short break in a restaurant on the summit and had a drink. My driver seemed to be a regular there and was immediately surrounded by many locals. I was already looking impatiently at my watch because I wanted to be at the hotel in Ouarzazate as soon as possible to meet up with Birgit and Markus. They had arrived the weekend before and would both be taking part in the Marathon des Sables for the third time. I was sure their company would help me dispel the last of my uncertainties and fears. We had already met twice in Zurich, and I was looking forward to meeting them again in Ouarzazate.

The driver finally noticed my impatience and gave me the signal that we would be going. The drive down the Anti-Atlas towards Ouarzazate was very impressive, too, and one sees the landscape transitioning to desert. The city is called "the gateway to the desert," and many desert tours and expeditions start from here. Ouarzazate combines the Amazigh words *ouar* (without) and *zazt* (noise), "the city without noise."

Ouarzazate is about 1,150 meters above sea level and was founded in 1928 by the French colonial administration. Once a garrison town of the French Foreign Legion, the city has one of the most renowned kasbahs of the country, Kasbah Taourirt. Ouarzazate is also referred to as the Hollywood of Morocco. Numerous films have been shot there, among them *Gladiator* and *The Mummy*, and most recently, some scenes from *Game of Thrones*. At the beginning of 2016, the first energy plant of what would become the world's largest solar thermal power site, called Noor, was completed just outside of Ouarzazate. It uses more than 500,000 parabolic mirrors.

After a bit more than 4 hours of driving, we finally reached my hotel for the next three nights, La Perle du Sud on Avenue

Mohammed V. The hotel has two stars and offers an ideal transition from the usual European way of life to the bivouac in the desert. At least that was Markus's opinion when he recommended the hotel to me, and he was right. Plus, everything was neat and clean.

After unpacking my bag, I joined Birgit and Markus at the pool. In the evening, the three of us had dinner in a local restaurant on Ouarzazate's main road. I had a vegetarian tajine, which I love. Often supplemented with meat and fruit, tajine is a vegetable stew, cooked slowly in a clay pot with a pointed lid. The vessel itself is also called tajine.

We spent a lot of time over the next two days lounging at the pool area in the courtyard of the hotel, Moroccan tea our constant companion. Short walks to the center of Ouarzazate were also part of our daily routine. The smells and noises of the city made me feel far away from my life back home.

I also used the time in Ouarzazate for two one-hour training runs. Running in the dry desert air was important because I wanted to get a feeling for my drinking plan a few times before going into the desert. This also gave me a sense of additional security.

Markus and I inspected our backpacks and their contents in the hotel's courtyard, unpacking and completely unfolding everything. Was there anything else to optimize? Markus destroyed the last grams of weight from his backpack that were not absolutely necessary, which mainly consisted of cutting away superfluous accessories and attachments. I didn't do that to avoid having straps that were too short.

Unexpectedly, I got a bit stressed trying to repack the backpack. It was difficult getting everything back into it. After working with all the items for a while, I finally managed to get it repacked. I also tried on my racing clothes again. I told myself over and over again that everything was going to be okay: the backpack and clothes would work just fine. The anticipation and the certainty that I would achieve my big goal and dream was rising. I would use the remaining time before the start for mental preparation.

On Friday morning, shortly after 8:00 a.m., a taxi picked us up at the hotel and drove us to the scheduled meeting place in front of the Hotel COS at the corner of Avenue Mohammed V and Avenue Moulay Rachid. We were not the first ones there, nor were we the last, and the tension in my body increased noticeably as the place filled with participants from all over the world, but the stress was joyful anticipation.

I got into a conversation with a female Dutch participant wearing Burberry patterned trousers. She had quite a lot of desert experience and was currently serving in a military mission in Mali. We talked about the peculiarities and dangers of the desert. It was a friendly and interesting conversation, like all the ones I would have during the coming week.

I boarded bus number 7 with Birgit and Markus, and we were bursting with excitement about where the journey would take us over the next few hours. I also recognized Elisabet Barnes on the bus, the female winner of the Marathon des Sables 2015, and she had ambitions to win the race again this year, as I had seen on her social media posts.

Directly in front of me in the luggage rack, I noticed a pair of prosthetic legs and saw that Duncan Slater was also on the bus. Duncan would become the first double leg amputee to complete the Marathon des Sables, the toughest footrace on earth. He lost his legs in 2009 in the Afghanistan war. Duncan had already achieved a degree of fame in 2013 for going on an expedition to the South Pole that included Prince Harry. The expedition and his start at the Marathon des Sables 2017 were connected with the fundraising campaign "Walking with the Wounded," a British charity that helps war veterans reintegrate back into society.

All of us runners departed in 25 buses for a location in the desert about 5 hours away. Where precisely that place was – it would be the place of our first bivouac and the start of the race – none of us knew until maps of the race were handed out after the buses left the city. My guess is that there are mainly two reasons for that: firstly, to keep it as a surprise, and secondly, for increased security by not disclosing the detailed route beforehand.

I couldn't believe my eyes when I saw a photo of my coach Timon climbing Jebel El Otfal on the cover of the roadbook. Since we were still in the suburbs of Ouarzazate with a connection to the cellular network, I pulled out my smartphone and immediately took a photo of the cover and sent it to Timon. He could hardly believe it and wished me all the best again by SMS. My coach on the cover of the roadbook – if that's not a good omen, then what is!

There were eager exchanges between novices and previous participants, and as I went through the roadbook, any remaining nervousness gave way to joyful anticipation.

At about the halfway point of the journey, the buses made a planned lunch stop, and we all received a lunch bag. I used the second half of the trip for a short power nap and dedicated most of the rest of the journey to the study of the roadbook.

At the beginning of the afternoon, we finally arrived at the first bivouac. The bivouac marshals immediately greeted us. Check-in was well organized, and we were soon guided to one of the Swiss tents that would be our home for the next eight nights.

NORTH EL MAHARCH
to
JEBEL EL MRAÏER

STAGE FOUR

STEPS AHEAD

Free.

Today is the long stage. The start time has been announced for 8:15 a.m., but like every morning, it will probably be somewhat delayed, which is one of those trivialities that I can't help but notice because it would bug me in my everyday life. But who cares if we reach the next bivouac 30 minutes later? There are no meetings that I need to attend. I am free from the obligations of my everyday life. This week gives me time to simply enjoy the desert with all its varied shades, colors, and moods.

There is a strict ban on mobile phones in the bivouac and on the route, and I appreciate this luxury of unattainability. In the bivouac, there is the possibility to write emails at certain times of the evening on fixed devices, but I have consciously decided to spare myself the trouble of queuing for a long time and prefer to use the available time for recreation and recovery. However, the organizer also offers the possibility to let family and friends at home send emails to your own inbox on the Marathon des Sables website, and the messages bring me great pleasure. The emails are delivered to our tent at about 8:00 p.m., and what could be nicer than reading the encouraging words of family and close friends before the night's rest. I'm quite overwhelmed by the amount of motivating emails I have received so far.

"You're great, sweetheart. I'm so proud of you! Rest well and know I'm thinking about you. Kisses, kisses, kisses!" – Monika

"Hello Daddy, we hope you're doing well! You now have already over half of it behind you and you'll master the rest of the days too. All the best!" – Simone and Danilo

"Hello Daddy, we hope you managed the first two stages well and your expectations were met. We wish you all the best for the rest of the week." – Manuela and Christian

"Hi Marcel, we keep our fingers crossed and wish you great experiences in the desert and fit legs." – Sabine and Martin

"Hey Marcel, now you have two stage-days behind you and a third is done soon! Keep it up and have many positive thoughts and experiences." – Anita and Aeneas

"Hi Marcel, you have already managed day one quite sovereignly. Keep it up! I send you a lot of energy!" – Brigitte

"Super Marcel, top performance! Keep up the good work and always listen well to your body. See you soon!" – Marco

"Hi Marcel, we hope everything is fine and you can make this run your very special experience and enjoy it. Do it well and see you soon! – Karin, Urs and Oliver

"Hello Honey, yesterday was a tough stage, right? I hope you recovered well and slept well. I think of you today and keep my fingers crossed. Do it well and I hug you tightly!" - Monika

Life has been reduced to the absolute necessities. Indeed, life at home, be it family or business, is going on without me, and I hope that is not to say that nobody misses me. I'm incredibly fascinated by the feeling of moving in a totally new environment, an isolated place void of the usual accouterments and trappings. In a way, I am making a journey to myself. Reflection has always been an essential element in my life, but this week is giving me more time than I have ever had before to think about the fundamental and important things in my life.

In the past, institutions such as the family, the church, or even schools have ensured that values and convictions were passed from generation to generation. Today, the passing on of values has become much more difficult as the structures of society have changed and are continuing to change, and adapting to change will remain our constant companion. The ongoing dialogue about values and principles in an increasingly digital and global world is important to me. Just as essential for me is regular self-reflection, and this is exactly what I want to do as much as possible in the desert.

I'm just about to start the long stage now. While waiting in the start corridor, I can't believe my eyes. A runner starts pissing on the ground right next to me and in the middle of a crowd of fellow runners. A small, frothy lake is forming in the sand, and that is something I do not want to step in.

Did this guy go completely crazy? I look at him quite shocked, and a loud curse leaves my mouth, and I'm not ashamed of it. He also gets well-deserved grimaces and slow head-shaking from the other runners around him. What kind of person is this man? Well, even such experiences, which one would rather not have, are made in the desert.

House to the right! After 3.5 kilometers I am passing a stone house. I have seen a few of these simple dwellings so far. Some seem to be inhabited, and others are in a somewhat decrepit, desolate state. Because of the sandy road that leads past the house, I assume people are living in it.

I am a little more nervous today than the days before. Not concerned, but just kind of nervous. I'm still in warming-up mode on today's 86.2 kilometers that is the long stage, the big test of the Marathon des Sables. According to the statistics of previous races – and common sense – the long stage sees the most dropouts. (There were 31 participants in total this year, and among them was Abdelkader El Mouaziz, the New York Marathon winner in 2000. As one of the favorites, I'm sure a DNF was not part of his plan.)

At the morning's pre-race briefing, we were told that hot temperatures are expected in the afternoon, which means that disciplined water and salt intake will be vital today, as they are every day. I will continue to adhere to two salt tablets per 1.5-liter bottle as I have been doing. There are still about 10 kilometers to reach the first checkpoint, and I am feeling strong.

From the start to the first checkpoint lies varied terrain, including the crossing of a sandy pass. Compared to passes in the Alps, which I know quite well from Switzerland, the pass is at a low elevation, but due to the deep, sandy ground, it is every bit as demanding as many of the passes I have crossed in my home country. I've been doing well so far. Looking ahead to today's stage, I tried to save some energy yesterday, especially towards the end of the stage, when I deliberately slowed down some. I was partly following the advice of former finishers, and partly I simply knew that it would pay off conserving some energy and fight for today's long stage.

Arriving at Checkpoint 1 with 13.6 kilometers and 1 hour and 52 minutes separating me from this morning's start, I again submit myself to the ritual that I will go through a total of 17 times during the week. I quickly scan the marked lanes for timekeeping and water delivery and line up in the one for my bib number and have a short chat with staff and volunteers.

"Are you okay, Marcel?"

"Yes, I am! Absolutely!"

I get 3 liters of fresh water and take a short rest in the shade of one of the off-road vehicles. Two bottles holding 3 liters of water are an unmistakable sign that the section to Checkpoint 2, which is only 10 kilometers, will have quite demanding terrain. I wager I will need almost 2 hours to tackle 10K!

I count my strides, 1 2 3 4 5 ... with a stride length of one meter, I cover 30 meters in 30 steps. If my stride length doubled with each step, I would circle the world 26 times in 30 steps. Exponential growth. I would then also reach the finish line of today's long stage shortly after completing 16 steps. But do I really want that? I am playing mathematics games in my head, something I love to do.

To enjoy every step in the Sahara and discover slowness is why I'm here. I probably circumnavigated our planet earth for the first time a few years ago and have run a total of 2,500 to 3,000 kilometers every year since.

The last 2 kilometers before reaching Checkpoint 2 are tough and sandy and absolutely hellish on my calves. They are catching fire. With nearly 60 kilometers in front of me, I know that mastering today's stage will be a big step. I am imagining how I will cross the finish line of the Marathon Stage on day six, which will be the next one, and visualize Patrick Bauer handing me the well-deserved finisher medal.

I'm still in control of myself, not even the smallest problem so far. Is that really possible? Could I really finish the race without blisters or other physical issues? The more I progress, the more I start to believe I can. I have a growing conviction that only an unexpected injury will prevent me from finishing, and I am convinced that such an injury is not in my destiny. At least not for this race.

I have mostly been spared significant injuries throughout my running life, and I do not want to familiarize myself with getting one here, which would be in one of the most inappropriate moments possible. My worst experience when it comes to injuries, as far as I can remember, was when I was as a young teenager at a scout camp in the Rhone Valley near Reckingen in the Swiss canton of Valais. Although I had been warned about climbing trees, I could not resist climbing one. I fell from a considerable height, and my left wrist landed on a stone. I heard the snap and immediately knew that something broke. And it wasn't the stone. There was no pain at first, probably because of shock, and I remember looking at my hand twisted at a wrong angle, and I thought it looked very odd. I wore a plaster cast for several months. The doctor said I had been very lucky.

To get through the desert unharmed is one of my main goals, and I run with great care and concentration, always looking closely during the technically difficult stretches.

I reach Checkpoint 2 at 23.7 kilometers in just past 3 hours and 49 minutes. I can feel the heat. It is the hottest day so far. The days before, I had always been back in the bivouac by the early afternoon. Today, the desert heat will be on me the entire day, and my plan sees me slowing down during the afternoon and probably even speed hiking for some time. Managing risks to secure a safe and successful finish is a priority. I know it will be a hot cruise to the next checkpoint, and I take some minutes in the shade of an off-roader to let my body cool down a little bit. But soon I'm on my way again. The terrain is mostly sandy as I pass a gorge. Heat accumulation below my safari cap is my constant companion, and I take it off regularly to let the air circulate. It's scorching now. Sunset will be at 7:42 p.m., and I am already looking forward to the cooler temperature.

Pictures of runners suffering from heatstroke that I saw on YouTube come to mind. I push them away and try to be positive. Positive thinking has made me strong in so many situations in my life, and why should I start having doubts about finishing the Marathon des Sables? No, I have no doubts. I will be a lucky finisher two days from now!

My safari cap comes off every couple of minutes. I am almost in a deep trance-like state. I am a part of every single moment. I let what is around me and what lies on the horizon affect me. I capture it all with my senses, and this prevents the emergence of any black thoughts that have drawn so many ultrarunners into a dark mental hole.

Some years ago, I read *Running with the Mind of Meditation: Lessons for Training Body and Mind*, the wonderful book by Sakyong Mipham, and it has given me a lot of inspiration. When the way ahead seems endless, sometimes counting up to one thousand and back helps, or counting in prime numbers, square numbers. The possibilities and choices are almost endless. I have been playing with numbers since my early childhood, and numbers are a steady companion.

It is mid-afternoon, and I have been on my way for 6 hours and 16 minutes when I arrive at Checkpoint 3. The sun burns and the heat is brutal. The long stage is as I expected it. There are many stories and legends about it, and I'm now fully dedicated to my own success story.

35.4 kilometers of the long stage are behind me, and there are another few hours of running in an oven in front of me until sunset. I am still sticking to my drinking plan, which works out to be an essential ritual, especially on this day. A sip of water every 5 minutes. Two salt tablets when opening a new 1.5-liter bottle. It's an obeisance to the sun god.

I decide I'll take a longer rest at the checkpoints from now on. Not that I feel I need to, but my desire to be a happy finisher tells me to give myself an added margin of comfort – though there is not going to be much comfort but rather less pain – and enough energy to see me through. With more than 50 kilometers to go, managing my energy level is going to be crucial.

Staying healthy is one of the highest goals in life. Being a gift, I do not take it for granted. The fact that I can still tackle a challenge like the Marathon des Sables at my age is a privilege I greatly appreciate. I am convinced that much in us, like the path of our lives, is predetermined, especially when it comes to health. Though I have read that a genetic test at an early age can tell you what to expect health-wise and allow you to react early with medication, I would reject such a test because it would be too much of a burden for me. I would not want to know, especially if I were a young man, that everything would potentially come to an end due to a predetermined illness. I will stick to a healthy diet and keeping the body in motion as the best prevention.

ULTRAMARATHON

Recalling how I found my way to ultra-races always brings a smile to my face. I have competed in over thirty marathons, but longer distances are my passion. Though any run that exceeds the classic marathon distance of 42.195 kilometers can technically be called an ultramarathon, there are different opinions, of course, as to which distance qualifies a run as an ultramarathon. I prefer to stay out of such discussions and do what I enjoy doing most, and that is running a long race in a beautiful landscape.

I remember very well my long-time running mate and friend, Aeneas Appius, asking me after my fifth finish of the Jungfrau-Marathon (one of the best-known mountain marathons in the world that takes place in the Swiss Alps), whether now would be the time for me to try out a longer distance. In his view, the Swissalpine Marathon, with start and finish in Davos, would be the ideal choice. Covering 78.5 kilometers, it was an icon of the European ultra trail scene.

At first, I could not imagine participating in such a race, but when Aeneas explained to me that the Swissalpine was even easier to run than the Jungfrau-Marathon, he had my ear. "The Swissalpine runs at a feel-good pace. It's a much easier pace than the Jungfrau," Aeneas insisted. "The only real difference is that it's much longer than a mountain marathon."

That was back in 2004. After listening to Aeneas, how could I not give running the Swissalpine serious consideration? I played with the idea of registering for it, and after a short consultation with my family, I decided to run it in 2005. I had to find out what it was like to run an ultra.

The Swissalpine Marathon has taken place annually since 1986. In addition to the K78 race of 78 kilometers, the event also includes several runs over shorter distances. The Swissalpine was the first ultra mountain run in Europe, and the second one, the legendary Swiss 100 kilometers of the Biel Running Days ultra-race, and both are perennial marks in the calendars of many ambitious ultrarunners.

After a break of thirteen years, the K78 returned to its original route over the Sertig Pass in 2010. I preferred the route over the Scaletta Pass with the magnificent Panorama Trail leading from Kesch-Hütte down to Scaletta, a matter of personal taste. The passage via Sertig Dörfli through the Sertig Valley down to the Landwasser Valley has its charm, too, although the course is not easy to run. The emotional highlight of both routes for me is, without a doubt, the passage by the Kesch-Hütte.

One year a jazz band was playing "When the Saints Go Marching In" in front of Kesch-Hütte, and it was as if they were playing it only for me. Such moments give me goosebumps and keep me training hard. I have finished the Swissalpine a total of seven times, and each race has its special history and place in my memories.

The Swissalpine is not overly challenging, and due to the way the course is mapped, it is rather easy to mentally break it up into specific segments. I ran the Swissalpine in 2012 for the last time. In 2013 I decided to participate in the newly established Eiger Ultra Trail in Grindelwald, where I have my beloved second home. In the years since, I have chosen to run the Eiger Ultra Trail and have never gone back to Davos. Meanwhile, the Eiger Ultra Trail has become one of the most asked about and highest-rated ultra-races in the world. It also belongs to the Ultra Trail World Tour. The mountains around Grindelwald are among the most beautiful Alpine landscapes in the world, and the view of them on the different courses is magical. There are four distances in total: the Ultra Trail, the supreme discipline, is 101 kilometers;

the Panorama Trail is 51 kilometers; the North Face Trail is 35 kilometers; last but not least, the Pleasure Trail is 16 kilometers. I have finished the long distance two times and the 51-kilometer Panorama Trail three times.

Because the Eiger Ultra Trail race weekend takes place in the middle of the summer, there is always the danger of thunderstorms. In 2015, after being on the trail for 16 hours and 40 minutes, I had intended to make only a short stop at Alpiglen. But when I wanted to set off again, it was no longer possible due to a violent thunderstorm. A race official said it was too dangerous with the pouring rain and flashing lightning, so we made ourselves comfortable in a cowshed that now served as a shelter for us runners. Arriving one after the other, all soaked to the bone, we were eventually a crowd of about twenty runners in the cowshed. The official said the forced interruption of the race could last up to two and a half hours. Safety first! Surprisingly, despite the obvious and immediate danger of the violent thunderstorm, some runners had difficulty accepting the correct and intelligent decision of the security commission to interrupt the race. It should also be mentioned that the Eiger Ultra Trail has one of the best, if not the best, safety and risk management systems in the ultra trail scene. OC President Ralph Näf had put his experience as a mountain guide of many years to use.

The time in the cowshed on Alpiglen was used to strike up new friendships and cultivate existing ones. Brigitte Daxelhoffer and Marco Baumann also arrived on Alpiglen shortly after me, so we were a group of three who knew each other. Last year, I had met Brigitte on the track here in Grindelwald for the first time, and Marco is a long-time friend of mine from Basel. Marco and I share one of my other passions, which is being an active participant in the Carnival of Basel and a member of one of its traditional societies. After the race started again, Marco and I covered the remaining distance to Grindelwald together, which officials had slightly shortened by then. We crossed the finish line hand in hand – it was captured in a photo by the official race photographer and has a place of honor in my photo collection.

Without a doubt, my finish of the Ultra-Trail du Mont Blanc in 2009 has a very special place in my memories too. The atmosphere in Chamonix on race weekend is magical and unbeatable. The authentic and tranquil mountaineering village becomes fully owned by ultrarunners. The fascinating thing about the UTMB, as it is abbreviated and colloquially called, is that you have a view of Mont Blanc throughout the entire race, assuming the weather allows it, of course. Over the 166 kilometers, runners circle the Mont Blanc mountain range, running through parts of France, Italy, and Switzerland and climbing almost 10,000 meters. A new experience for me was being up on my feet through two nights: the race started at 6:30 p.m. on Friday, and I crossed the finish line on Sunday shortly after 2:00 p.m. It was the longest I had ever gone without sleep. Inevitably, as experienced UTMB participants had told me, hallucinations crept up on me during the second night: tree roots turned into talking dwarfs, and the backpacks of other participants in front of me became grim faces. It caused me some fear and discomfort at the beginning, but it is apparently harmless as long as one still knows that it is merely a matter of misperception. At least that is what I learned from my wife after she spoke about it with our daughter, Manuela, who was already studying medicine by then. I have to admit that the real reason for calling Manuela was the fact that I saw creatures moving across the ceramic plates on the walls in our hotel bathroom when taking my usual hot after-race bath.

During the UTMB, all the inhabitants of the region around Chamonix seemed to come out for the race. Thousands of spectators were celebrating and applauding us runners at the start. *"Bon courage, bon courage"* echoed through the narrow streets of Chamonix as we made our way through the village; Vangelis's "Conquest of Paradise" joined in from the many loudspeakers alongside the main street. At the checkpoint and refreshment post in Saint Gervais, a grandiose cheese buffet awaited us. Something else I remember as if it were yesterday was the big herd of Alpine ibex I encountered on a shoulder of rock during the descent from Col du Bonhomme. Being born on December 25 under the zodiac sign Capricorn, of course it was a special moment for me. And there was Bovine, a hamlet 2,000 meters above sea level. After what felt like an almost endless and incredibly steep ascent, passing through a lane of torches during the last meters to the refreshment post was something that can hardly be surpassed mystically or emotionally.

The UTMB was an experience that can still jerk my emotional strings with its many images and feelings. It left a wonderful nub on my memories and continues to anchor me positively at crucial moments. I would go so far as to say that running the UTMB helps me with mastering many difficult situations I find myself in by creating a needed energy boost. Run the UTMB, and you'll know that you can always find untapped energy inside you. Running gives so much to take with you.

I went back to the Chamonix region another time in 2018 to run the CCC, which stands for Courmayeur-Champex-Chamonix. The CCC's 101 kilometers follow the second part of UTMB's route, and in my memories of it, I'm basically left with scattered images of running in brutal weather. I was a lucky finisher in the end, I suppose.

Having finished 14 ultramarathons, I was ready to tackle the Marathon des Sables adventure with some solid experience under my elastic waistband. There had been some forced dropouts as well, but I always emerged, in the end, given some time, strengthened. As the American bestselling author and leadership expert John Calvin Maxwell once said, "Sometimes you win, sometimes you learn." It is one of the principles I try to live by.

Another long-cherished wish became a reality in 2018 when I took part in the 100 kilometers of Biel. Having a bike companion in Biel has a long tradition, and Aeneas accompanied me on his bike. Legendary German runner and author Werner Sonntag said, *"Irgendwann musst du nach Biel"* (At some point you have to go to Biel.), which was also the title of one of his books. But finishing in Biel was quite painful for me in the end, and I have to accept that running 70 kilometers on concrete takes more specific preparation. Next time!

After all these years of running, I have learned to listen carefully to my body. I run without a heart rate monitor and trust myself to determine my heart rate accurately to within about five beats. The holistic management of my energy is important because I travel a lot in my job and long work hours are more the rule than the exception, which often makes it necessary to readjust my training. On the flip side, the frequent travel for work has opened up different perspectives of places, and I usually schedule longer sessions on days when I've spent the night in a foreign city. I get up early, something I never have problems with, and am often one of the very first to appear in the parks along with the rising sun. Hyde Park in London, Tiergarten in Berlin, Stadtpark in Vienna, Central Park in New York, Lakefront Trail in Chicago, Parque del Retiro in Madrid. I have explored all of them and many more, gaining insights that I never would have had by staying in bed in my hotel room. I was in Central Park in early 2005 on the day "The Gates" installation by Bulgarian artist Christo and French artist Jeanne-Claude was being dismantled. Small strips of the deep saffron-colored nylon fabric panels that decorated paths of Central Park for over 37 kilometers were being cut out and given to passers-by. I was lucky enough to get hold of one that has served as a bookmark ever since. It is a nice memory from one of my favorite running spots.

I don't know how long I will be able to compete in ultra-races. I just want to enjoy it as long as I can. And what will happen when this joy and passion is taken away from a body that has been programmed to move for so many years? I assume it should probably happen gradually. It will be a long goodbye.

I do know that a hike on a beautiful autumn day together with my wife will always give me the joy and satisfaction I need.

STAGE FOUR

NIGHTFALL

I'm somewhere between Checkpoints 4 and 5 and sunset is approaching. The air has started to feel cooler, and soon I will cover my arms to avoid my body cooling down too fast. The changing terrain and lots of stones on the ground tell me to be careful with each step. With the sun moving down in front of me, the atmosphere can hardly be described in words. The field of runners is widely spread out across a plain. After nearly 10 hours since starting at the bivouac this morning, the space between runners is growing. I'm falling into a sensitive mood, overwhelmed by the beauty. Thoughts and memories come and go. I see pictures that have shaped my life as clear as if it had been yesterday: the early years with Manuela and Simone; all the memorable places around the world I've been to on family travels and business trips; my first marathon finish.

A tear rolls down my cheek. Some years ago, Mom had gone away forever. It took me a long time to overcome and accept her death. The last years we shared are often with me. She was seriously ill for a couple of years. I knew death was redemption for her, but that doesn't mean too much when you lose someone so close to you. The loss hurts.

I'm rolling over small dunes. It might sound easy, but my experience is that it is pretty tough. Burning muscles come and go. Not even one cramp so far this week: what a lucky runner I am! Or is it rather a sign that my carefully prepared nutrition plan is paying off? It seems so, and for me, this is another proof point that preparation that focuses on every detail is essential for successfully participating in – and finishing – an adventure like the Marathon des Sables.

It is dark now; twilight felt pretty short. I can feel the air rapidly cooling. The big difference in day and night temperatures is typical for deserts. Two factors contribute to the difference: a clear sky leads to a higher increase of daytime temperatures; the structure of the desert surface means heat is only stored in the upper layers, so heat escapes quickly at night.

I decided to run the Marathon des Sables without musical accompaniment. The decision was made on the first night in the bivouac. I wanted to concentrate all my senses on the desert's charms, and I believe that this was the right decision. Nevertheless, at certain moments like this one, I would be happy to be able to dive into my favorite music for at least a few minutes: Van Morrison's masterpiece *Astral Weeks*, Bruce Springsteen's *Born to Run*, and Bob Dylan's *Blood on the Tracks* to mention a few. Also, a jazz album belonging to some of my all-time favorites would be a pleasure: Eddie Harris's *Last Concert* and Keith Jarret's *Köln Concert* are way up there.

Although jazz is a passion of mine, I rarely listen to jazz while running. I enjoy the rich phrases, the tones and tunes, whether at concerts or playing favorites from my collection at home. I have dedicated significant time outside of business to jazz, and I would say that jazz has become intertwined with my life. For 10 years I've been engaged in organizing jazz concerts, and bringing together jazz musicians has afforded me a unique opportunity and privilege that perhaps I haven't appreciated enough. Many of the people I have met, musicians, music directors and jazz fans like myself, have become friends, and we exchange thoughts about things that go well beyond music, and that's something that has given me perspectives I wouldn't otherwise have gained by just moving around in my business circles. Jazz is not a style, nor is it a rhythm: it is communication, improvisation, innovation, and self-expression in a moment of time, as Miles Davis once said. As in business, communication is a crucial element of jazz.

I arrive at Checkpoint 5. There are still 30 kilometers in front of me, which I try to see as one of the many long runs I did during my preparation over the last months. If I add the upcoming Marathon Stage, I'm 72 kilometers away from getting my medal and a deserved hug from Marathon des Sables founder Patrick Bauer, who does that with each and every finisher. The final ranking happens after the Marathon Stage, but the last short stage over the fantastic Erg Chebbi dunes is still mandatory if you are to be an overall finisher. For the first time, I'm now sure that only an injury can prevent me from realizing my more than 25-year-old dream.

Checkpoint 5 has a setup that looks a bit like a mix between a refreshment post and a beach club. Lounge chairs are spread around – Marathon des Sables branded, of course – where runners take the opportunity to relax for a couple of minutes. I do the same and spend a good quarter of an hour sitting down for the first time in more than 11 hours. Since nobody will probably believe me when I talk about it at home, I take a couple of photos of us runners lounging. We look like we are at the beach except that there is no water and we are dirty and look worn out.

Ready to go now. When it comes to terrain, the next part of the long stage will be one of the toughest and most challenging of the whole week. I will have to run nearly 8 kilometers through high dunes with the moon watching me. My headlamp gives me all the light I need. I have set it at the lowest level because there was a full moon only two days ago, and the moonlight drapes the Sahara in a mystical, illuminated dress.

All of a sudden I'm hearing grunting noises coming from close by. Approaching the sounds, I make out the silhouettes of a small herd of camels. I count more than 10 of them. Camels and the desert are inseparable from each other for me, but these are the first wild ones I have met since arriving in the Sahara. Camels living in the Sahara have only one hump and are called dromedaries. They are the tallest of the camel species and still serve an important function in the desert. They do far more than carrying tourists through the dunes: the salt caravans, connecting the southern Sahara and Sahel, still play an important role in exchanging goods, and they still use dromedaries. The name of the dromedary goes back to the Greek word *dromas*, which means running. I say goodbye to my four-legged fellow runners and move on towards Checkpoint 6.

Shortly after somebody shouts, "Salut, Marcel!" and I turn back and see Alain, a member of the Swiss group a few tents over from ours. Most of them live in the French part of Switzerland called la Romandie. Alain belongs to the group of the fastest runners who started 3 hours after us this morning. It took him about 60 kilometers to catch me. What a performance! I say "chapeau" to him, and we talk for a few minutes before he moves off at his pace. Alain is a winegrower and runs the family business on Lake Geneva. That's what I like so much about ultrarunning: you meet people from such diverse backgrounds and professions, which feeds life with a lot of inspiration.

As I watch Alain move off, the paradox of Achilles and the tortoise comes to mind. It is said that the ancient Greek philosopher Zeno of Elea tried to prove that in a race, a fast runner like Achilles can never catch up to a tortoise if he gives it a head start. His reasoning is that by the time Achilles has reached the starting position of the tortoise, the tortoise has already moved on, and there is a new, smaller gap between the two, and this goes on and on the same way. The gap between Achilles and the tortoise may become infinitesimally small as time goes on, but there will always be a gap, and Achilles will never truly catch up to the tortoise. Zeno's argument is fascinating, but it must be a fallacy since, of course, a faster runner will always catch up to the slower one. Zeno does not consider that summing up an infinite amount of numbers (in this case, the gaps) can return something finite.

I have already passed Checkpoint 6 and the field of runners is widely spread out. At one point, I can't see anybody around me and have obviously lost my way. The sticks that mark the route have lost most of their luminosity, but since the runners all have their headlights on, it is easy enough getting back on the route. In case I do become lost in the desert, I could use my compass plus the information included in the roadbook to find my way to the next checkpoint. Some field tests at home with my compass were also part of my race preparation. You never know! On top of that, we all wear a GPS device that would allow a rescue team to find us in case of an emergency.

My body's fuel tank is starting to run on empty with a bit more than 15 kilometers to the finish line. I pass one last checkpoint and soon see the lights of the bivouac in the distance. I'm getting slower now, and the battery of my headlamp is also running low.

When I cross the finish line, my watch shows 17:49:47.

What an emotional moment. The legendary long stage of the Marathon des Sables is behind me!

The mint tea never tasted so good. I spend some time just beyond the finish line absorbing the atmosphere in the finishing area. Runners are scattered around or sitting in the sand, and they all seem to be entirely within themselves. Overwhelmed by intense emotions, I recognize that this is a moment of great height and depth for me. I watch runners approach the bivouac with their shining headlights. Everybody arriving looks filled with happiness and bubbling with endorphins. It is a scene that I know I will remember for a long time to come.

As I make my way to tent number 35, I can feel every little stone under my feet. This is the usual sensitivity after an ultra-race. It is the first time I make the short walk to our tent in darkness, with only a bit of shining light from the tents around me since my headlight switched off after the battery died shortly after I crossed the finish line. I had read that there are scorpions that come out at night to hunt, but so far only a few have been seen. These are thick-tail scorpions and are not too poisonous. Rather rare are deathstalker scorpions, one of the most dangerous species of scorpions. They can be fatal to humans. I pray that I won't see any of these during the week. For the unlikely event of getting a venomous scorpion or insect bite, all of us must carry an anti-venom pump.

I reach my tent where Ricarda, Jens, and Simon are expecting me. Before saying our goodnights, we agree to go to the finish line after a couple of hours of sleep to cheer arriving runners. The last ones are expected after 6:00 p.m., the absolute deadline of 35 hours. As a nice tradition, all runners come out to cheer the very last runner who crosses the line. It will be Jan Taylor, a woman from New Zealand, welcomed by a compatriot singing the national anthem. Goosebumps!

THE BIVOUAC EXPERIENCE

Our accommodation in the desert consisted of a Berber tent of the simplest design. The Berber nomads in the Maghreb states lived in such tents a long time ago, and some still do today. What particularly impressed me about our *home* during a total of eight desert nights was the simplicity and practicality of the Berber tent. Mainly made of goat and camel hair, a Berber tent is a simple blanket used as a tarp and stretched over several wooden poles. Two long poles provide stability in the middle section, and shorter poles further stabilize the sides and allow optimum use of the interior. The tent is then secured against wind or storms by iron pegs laboriously hammered into the rock-hard desert ground. The tent floor is covered with a carpet, and it is up to the tent inhabitants arriving first after each stage to clean the underlying floor from stones and smooth out uneven areas.

We had already organized who would be in our tent on the bus trip to the first bivouac – the organizer distributed lists in the buses for the registration of desired tent mates. Since Birgit, Markus, Ricarda, Jens, and I had already agreed in advance that we would share a tent, everything went smoothly and quickly. On the way to the bivouac, we also picked up Simon, which in the end brought us to six people, which was two less than a full tent. There was still the chance that the organizer would allocate more athletes to our tent, but we lucked out, and that did not happen. The additional space was much appreciated.

After leaving the bus, Markus briefed us that we should go to the check-in immediately so that we could choose the tent that was closest to the entrance of the bivouac from the tents that were allocated to Switzerland, all placed consecutively at the inner ring of the bivouac. He said we could save up to a kilometer of walking per day, which would save us energy. The bivouac was arranged in three circles and consisted of a total of 166 tents. The inner ring was comprised of 50 tents and the outer 60.

With Markus, we had an experienced Marathon des Sables participant and tent builder among us, which turned out to be an inestimable advantage several times during the week. For example, Markus knew exactly how to rearrange the geometry of the tent to prevent unpleasantness when the wind changed and sandstorms approached. Yes, sometimes it even seemed that he could almost read the weather long before strong winds or an abrupt change of wind direction became noticeable. If a strong wind came up, objects and running gear from other tents would fly around, and it was usually as much of a game trying to grab other people's things as it was holding the tent together and preventing it from flying away in a Saharan storm. We were lucky that we were spared from any big sand storms in 2017.

During the night, the tent side facing the wind is always folded down. But during the day, it is advisable to keep the long sides of the tent as open as possible so that the air flowing through has a cooling effect.

It was an extraordinary experience for me how we became virtually one with our tent over the days. In a short time everything went smoothly. Participants spent two nights in the tent before the start of the race, which helped all of us to adjust to our new accommodations and the desert climate and conditions. The first night in particular allowed me to try out different arrangements of my clothes and equipment. I also used it to test my sleeping pad and inflatable pillow. Until then, I hadn't known what it felt like to spend a whole night on the inflatable mattress that was deliberately too short, with a length of only 119 centimeters: I had decided to save some additional grams of weight. But would I be able to find adequate sleep on the hard desert floor?

Furthermore, what was the effective added value of the inflatable mini pillow of a well-known Swiss mountain equipment manufacturer? Well, getting used to the inflatable mattress was useful and necessary. With a width of only 51 centimeters, it was far from what you would call a luxury bed. So it was unavoidable that during the night – and this was the case during the whole week – I would be on and off the carpet with one leg or even a little more of my body. But in the end it was pretty much okay, and I definitely decided to keep the sleeping pad for the week out in the desert. As for the pillow, it should be mentioned that I had filled it a bit too much with air the first night. I corrected that the next night and wanted it under my head from then on.

I was already in a good sleep rhythm the first nights, though it was not an uninterrupted deep sleep of several hours. Despite what was predominantly light sleep, I always had the feeling that I was sufficiently rested in the morning and was ready for the day's challenge. I also think that my body had automatically switched into some kind of standby mode early in the morning: my mind was focused on the upcoming race.

Each runner has to find his or her own best sleeping configuration. My tent mate, Jens, for example, a somewhat experienced desert runner, had completely renounced sleeping pads, but you could also see some participants carrying real monster sleeping mats. For me, it was important right from the start that all the gear that I had to carry around the whole week could be stored inside my backpack. I wanted to avoid having things attached to the outside constantly knocking against the backpack. This was one of the really valuable tips that Marco Jaeggi had given me.

The process after crossing the finish line of any stage almost always followed the same ritual. Immediately after the finish I would go directly to our tent, number 35, which was located at the same place every time the bivouac was rebuilt. I would then change into my bivouac clothes: a pair of sports shorts and my second running shirt. That was, so to speak, my "evening dress."

I unpacked my inflatable sleeping pad and pumped air into it with all the energy I still had at my disposal. Then I made myself comfortable and enjoyed an hour of recovery.

Marco Jaeggi called this time the "golden hour," and the first hour after arrival in the bivouac was absolute quality time for me. I mostly fell into a short power nap, which did me a lot of good. Then I would make an inspection of my body, especially my feet. I removed any grains of sand with a lot of patience. And then I had a protein drink for regeneration.

In the course of the afternoon, all of us would be together in the tent, except for the long stage on the fourth day when the arrival of our little tent tribe was spread out over a more extended period of time.

After the "golden hour," it was time to collect wood. Yes, that's correct, gathering wood in the desert! For the preparation of dinner, each of us built individual fires. While I was content with one dry fuel tablet per evening meal, Simon preferred to make his fire with wood, so of course we all helped collect firewood and stones to build a shield against the wind.

We all fell into our own rhythm in the evening. While some were still busy eating dinner, others were already getting into their sleeping bags. Sunset was at about 7:45 p.m., and darkness fell suddenly. In those minutes I could hear every little noise around me, no matter how low. The crackling of flames in the middle of the bivouac where a fire was lit every evening triggered marvelous feelings in me, and one time I found myself back in my early scout days as a teenager. Strong emotions arose. Last shimmers of light drew the landscape far off in the horizon in razor-sharp contours. Then Simon's fire would go out, and our tent would sink into an almost ghostly silence.

Though we took an evening toilet before going to sleep, I usually had to get once more during the night. Since there was a full moon in the middle of the race week, the bivouac was at this time – mostly around 2:00 a.m. – brightly illuminated. A lamp was not even necessary. Snoring from surrounding tents, more or less discrete, accompanied me on my way to pee.

From a simple iron frame, spanned with tent tarpaulins, was a block of three simple toilets. A few of these blocks were distributed around the bivouac on the outer ring at a distance of about 50 meters from the tents. In each of the stalls was a toilet seat, and of course, it was without a drain. At the end of every stage, the organizer provided two compostable bags, which were then stretched over the toilet seat. After knotting the bag, you dropped it in a waste bin from where it was disposed of by the staff into a hole far outside the bivouac. Within five days, the *shit* is supposed to dissolve. In the early morning and in the late evening, veritable queues formed in front of the toilet tents, and it was difficult to avoid them because the rhythm of the body seemed to be the same for nearly everybody.

Another challenge was the daily washing of the body. About one liter of water had to suffice, which would have been unimaginable for me before my time in the desert. Following Markus's tip, I crafted my own little shower gadget that turned out to be indispensable. With my pocket-knife, a mandatory item, I perforated the cap of a PET bottle, filled the bottle with the desired amount of water, put the cap back on, and the simplest shower in the world was ready to be used. Amazingly, it always felt like a luxury when I used it!

The bivouac experience is something I will always remember as it forms an important part of the overall Marathon des Sables experience. Even today, all my senses can capture the special ambiance of the bivouac, and it always gives me a longing for the desert. Then I often feel melancholy and have a strong urge to be back there again.

JEBEL EL MRAÏER
to
MERDANI

STAGE FIVE

HIGHWAY TO HELL

So close.

I used the free day after the long stage to recover for the upcoming Marathon Stage, which is the only remaining true challenge before my successful finish of the Marathon des Sables.

I am so close now!

My coach Timon had told me that life in the bivouac is about lolling around, resting, and eating, and that's exactly what I did during the rest day. *Dolce far niente*! I didn't count, but I think I scattered about five power naps throughout the day. Power napping is something I needed to learn. It takes me a very short time to fall asleep, and I always wake up after about 30 to 45 minutes. It is not really a deep sleep, but it noticeably replenishes my body and mind. My inner clock has never let me down, and as I've mentioned before, I have never overslept in my whole life. But I sure wish I could have overslept on rest day.

During the rest day I also went to the finish line a few times to cheer for the still incoming finishers of the long stage. Incredibly, the last arriving runners needed about twice the time I did, or 35 hours. What an accomplishment and what an effort! Another nice tradition of the Marathon des Sables is that everybody applauds all the runners as they pass the inner circle of the bivouac to reach their tents.

I also prepared a big treat for myself: macaroni and cheese! What a wonderful dish that was, and it really was the reward it was meant to be. I had planned to have it as a late breakfast, and that is exactly what it was. Like everything I took with me, I had tested it before, and I find it amazing how high-tech food producers manage to create such high-quality meals. Okay, it is not the same as at my favorite Italian restaurants, but I felt such joy when opening the vacuum pack. Maybe I could add some oven-dried guanciale next time. It would be a few grams of extra weight, but I would value the reward. Guanciale is my favorite ingredient for a tasty carbonara dish. It is cured bacon-like meat derived from *guancia*, which is the Italian word for cheek.

The rest day turned out to be among the hottest of the week, and I spent as much time as possible in the shade of our tent. We kept it open on both sides during the whole day, letting the wind circulate for a comfortable climate. Friendships form among tentmates during the week, and in our tent of six, we will all know a substantial part of everyone's life story by the time we leave Morocco in a few days. We had a lot of time to chat, especially during the rest day, and it seems that the more days we spend together, the more our conversations take a philosophical turn.

Today's start has been set for 7:00 a.m. and is the earliest start of the week. The Marathon Stage is not called that by accident: the distance in the roadbook is exactly 42.2 kilometers, the distance of a marathon. But here in the remote desert, AIMS, the organization that usually measures the accuracy of a marathon race, was not involved, and thus I assume that in the end we will run a few meters more or less. Nothing more than a small triviality.

It's time for Patrick Bauer to climb atop the off-road vehicle like every morning for the usual pre-race briefing. The last part of America's "Horse With No Name" slowly fades as Patrick announces another hot day, which I expected after the temperatures I felt during yesterday's rest day. One last challenging day. I feel good. I feel very good. Despite the rather cold nights, I have been spared any signs of a cold probably owed to my body knowing that a cold is not really an option out here in the desert. Mental strength!

The pack of runners is ready to go, and I can feel the anticipation of the emotions of finishing today's stage all around. This will be it! Even "Highway to Hell" seems louder than the days before.

> "Living easy, living free, season ticket on a one-way ride…
> I'm on the highway to hell, on the highway to hell
> Highway to hell, I'm on the highway to hell."

Rock history!

It's worth mentioning that the famous AC/DC song has been my ringtone since I signed up for the Marathon des Sables and still is. A few times when I forgot to put my phone on silent mode, it has gone off during business meetings. One time was during a board meeting that I myself was chairing. Funny stories that make up the experience of participating in a Marathon des Sables.

A loud bang and Patrick sends us off on Stage 5. We move through the beautiful small dunes that were in front of our bivouac for the rest day. After 1.5 kilometers we reach a stony plateau, and the next part of the race leads us along crevassed and rugged riverbeds. A dried-out lake and a branch of an *oued* are my companions for the last 2 kilometers before I reach the first checkpoint. I look at my Suunto watch and it shows 1:06:09 after 10.5 kilometers. I know that it is probably a bit too fast, but starting too fast is something I often do in races. I also have never managed to have a negative split in a marathon, which would be running the second half faster than the first. Even when I ran my personal best in Hamburg in 2002 with a time of 2:56:48, the second half took me a few minutes longer. I decide to consciously slow down my speed since there are still more than 30 kilometers to cover, 30 hot kilometers. After the water ritual I only take a short rest as I want to cover as much ground as possible during the relatively cool morning.

The distance between the checkpoints is 11.7 kilometers with quite varied terrain. At about kilometer 16, crossing a slightly stony plateau, I can see a bunch of houses not too far off to my left. It is Taouz, with its distinctive broadcasting tower and a date palm oasis belonging to a rural commune. I cross another riverbed and feel my calves burning, and another stony plateau and its done. I'm at Checkpoint 2 after 2 hours and 35 minutes.

It is obvious that I'm more preoccupied with time and listening to my body today than before. The simple reason is the ambition to have everything under control and minimize all risks during this important day. The good news is that I'm feeling good. Really good! The closer I get to the finish line, the more I feel like I'm flying high. Endorphins! I know their feel-good effect from many of my runs over the last 20 years, and it is an unmistakable sign that I'm part of something much bigger. At least that is kind of what I feel in such moments. I more or less flew through Checkpoint 2, and as I was about to set off, I saw my tent mate Simon arriving, and we agree to run together for some time.

When we leave the checkpoint, I know that there is less than a half marathon in front of me. I try to see it like one of my shorter long runs during preparation. Without the burning sun, I would say it would be a piece of cake. After a couple of kilometers running together, Simon and I say goodbye. It is important to find your own pace in such a race, and he has decided he wants to go a bit faster.

About half of the distance between Checkpoints 2 and 3 is through dunes. Patrick Bauer is famous for finding the right challenges for us runners, even during the last stages. My legs have taken me over more than 200 kilometers of the Sahara, and these dune passages should be the last remaining big test for them. My legs have served me well. I consciously take it easy in the dunes and arrive at Checkpoint 3 after 4 hours and 49 minutes. I'll learn later that Simon had passed the checkpoint about 24 minutes earlier. He was obviously successful in fighting the dunes. There are 8.5 kilometers left until the finish line now, and I know they will be hot ones.

On a sandy passage through the hills, I switch between running and speed hiking. A runner is about 100 meters ahead, and another runner is about 100 meters behind. I use the silence to ponder what is important.

A few years ago I had a discussion with a friend about what constitutes a good person as a family man, friend, member of society. Soon the conversation started to revolve around our children, and we realized how important it is to have a stabilizing influence on their development in today's fast-paced world. I consider the handover and transmission of values and principles to our daughters to be one of the most important tasks of Monika and me as parents. Teaching one's children everything they need to master their own lives successfully requires a lot of time and sometimes just as much strength.

My friend then made a remark that touched me close to the heart and became somewhat of a guiding principle in my dealings with our daughters. "You know, Marcel," he said, "for me it was very important in the upbringing of my children that they should never forget where their roots are, but that we also needed to succeed in giving them wings at the right moment and enabling them to go their own way. And I want them to know that they can come back at any time if they need support and advice."

I have often reflected on these thoughts since then. Both Manuela and Simone had left our house relatively early, and I wouldn't be honest if I didn't mention that I had suffered a lot at the beginning when they left.

I arrive at M'Fis, a small mining outpost, at kilometer 37.4 and am less than 5 kilometers from the bivouac where we will stay for the last night. I can already see the bivouac from here. The M'Fis mining area is rich in minerals, especially barite. The work is still done in a very old-fashioned way by using trenches. Time seems to stand still here. The village has been deserted for some time and exudes a somewhat morbid albeit charming atmosphere.

I capture the moment and the morbid charm of this place with my camera.

Here in the desert I tend to take a few photos every time I unpack my digital camera, sand-proof and lightweight at only 148 grams including spare battery. When I was a boy and a young man, waiting for the best moment was part of being a passionate photographer. To shoot a masterpiece, you had to be willing to wait, you needed patience and had to observe the target. Back then you wouldn't see the result for days or even weeks until the film was developed. And I was a passionate plane spotter at the time as well, so I'm sure many of my old photographs hold rare aviation moments. Taking a shot was a conscious process because there was always a price tag behind every photo. This changed totally when the first digital cameras came out in the early 90s. I have more than 20,000 photos on my smartphone, a multiple of all the photographs I took with my film cameras. And if I'm honest, this is probably something between nonsense and wastefulness. It's just because storage doesn't really have a price tag anymore.

In the course of our lives, we adapt quickly to new developments, and photography is only one example where the effect goes far beyond technology. It often also changes our behavioral patterns, sometimes for the better and sometimes for the worse.

I leave M'Fis and feel like flying down the remaining 4 kilometers to the bivouac.

A couple of hundred meters from the finish, I see Patrick Bauer cheering on the incoming runners and awarding them their well-deserved medals. I get goosebumps again.

And now it's my turn. I get a big hug from Patrick as I pass the finish line with a time of 6:06:12, and I feel like a real champion.

I did it! What an unbelievable feeling. I feel joy and pride as I walk towards the mint tea station, tears rolling down my cheek as I let my emotions go. I stop for some minutes to anchor the moment in my memory. Once again, the mint tea never tasted so good. As I walk to our tent I'm overwhelmed by emotions and spontaneously give high fives to a couple of other runners. When I arrive at our tent, I see a lot of joy in the faces of Ricarda, Jens, and Simon. We hug each other tightly and share the experiences of the day.

Birgit and Markus arrive safely later in the afternoon, and both are in good shape. It is a certainty that our whole group will successfully finish this year's Marathon des Sables. Between now and the arrival in Merzouga, where we will be picked up by buses, tomorrow will be more of a promenade through the dunes. That's what former finishers are saying, and Jens and Markus are two of them.

The last bivouac is set up just at the foot of the wonderful Erg Chebbi dunes. I have seen few things in my life that compete with its natural beauty. Erg is derived from the Arabic word *irq*, which translates to "sand sea," and the Erg Chebbi is one of two big ergs in the Moroccan Sahara. The dunes cover nearly 100 square kilometers, and many rise up over 150 meters. The color of the sand appears to change depending on the weather and time of day.

The bivouac lies close to the Algerian border, the closest we've been during the week. I think about the four Swiss tourists who were abducted in the Algerian part of the Sahara about 15 years ago. I can still remember the discussions in the media after the liberation of the Swiss tourists about who, in the end, should bear the costs. The insurance company, the state, or the liberated themselves? I was a bit alienated by those discussions since, in my humble view, this is not as important as the people being freed.

I am not afraid of being kidnapped. We are guarded around the clock by military men who are not visible to us. The Marathon des Sables is under the patronage of the Moroccan king, and that gives me a heightened sense of security. I'm looking into the distance, and for a split second, I think I see a guard sheltering far away on a little dune.

As the traditional protocol goes, there is a party in the evening after the Marathon Stage. And guess what? We also will get a beer or soft drink as a special reward. But there is only one per runner, which is strictly monitored as everything has been during the whole event. There is also the award ceremony awaiting and a musical surprise. I heard that last year part of the Paris Opera Orchestra played under the moon and stars. And I have to say that I'm a bit disappointed that it is a female French rock singer this year. She is good, no doubt about it, but I would have preferred classical music that would have emphasized the brilliance of this place in the desert much better, at least in my view. Nevertheless, it is an unforgettable evening with the moon and stars lighting the big dunes behind the bivouac and creating a magical atmosphere. After we cheered this year's overall winners, Elisabeth Barnes and Rachid El Morabity, and the winners of the different age categories, I slowly make my way back to our tent, where I want to experience a few moments of silence by myself.

Shortly after I fall asleep.

NOTES ON RUNNING

It was never my ambition to win races. My relative performance has improved, and steady learning cycles have helped me improve my running. Today, I could claim to run fast times in my age group, but that is not so important to me.

Running ultra-races, at times, feels like I'm on a rollercoaster. It can be tough and often makes me think about the reasons why I run. Why do I put on my running shoes no matter how horrible the weather is? Why volunteer for such suffering, especially when a previous night's over-exuberance still has a stranglehold on my body? Well, trail running has developed into probably the most meaningful part of my life besides my family and professional responsibilities. I can hardly imagine a life without it, which is especially noticeable when I have to stay away from running for a longer time due to an injury or illness, which fortunately doesn't happen often. I don't feel well balanced without it. *"Mens sana in corpore sano,"* as the Roman poet Juvenal said nearly 2,000 years ago.

A smooth sea never made a skilled sailor.

Franklin D. Roosevelt

Pain comes and goes, but success lasts, and so too does giving up. As I would never give up a race because of mental or physical pain – within limits, of course – just as I would not give up on any situation in life as long as there is a chance, however slim, that it will succeed. And one trait that repeatedly helps me overcome misfortunes and mastering every-day challenges is my resilience. My initial awakening to the power of resilience was some years ago at a two-day workshop facilitated by my long-time mentor Karsten Drath. I learned a lot about my traits and how to train my habits at the workshop. Over time, my resilience increased, making me able to counterbalance extraordinary and challenging situations with actions based on my skills and resources. Running can be an excellent training field to alter undesired habits and further develop positive ones. "Excellence is an art won by training and habituation," as Aristotle said. Being able to react to a particular situation with the right habit has definitely helped me to cope better with problems in running as well as day-to-day life. I have established my own methods to tackle, survive, and even triumph in unexpected situations. Counting stones and trees or focusing on the plants around me while detecting the order of the leaves (I'm fascinated by the Fibonacci sequence) and their individual characteristics are some examples from running. I engage myself mentally in something outside the immediate troubling and disturbing situation to keep my mind focused. It helps me to win back the energy and mental conviction that a given goal is still achievable.

> **The significance of a man is not in what he attains but in what he longs to attain.**
>
> Kahlil Gibran

There isn't no such thing as a "free lunch" in life, and we should not expect to receive something for nothing, without making an effort. From time to time we might get lucky, but as a general rule, accomplishing goals and reaching dreams takes a lot of hard work, and that is especially true in ultrarunning. Knowing how it feels to reach a goal creates an incredible amount of energy to fight for a new one. When I commit to a new running project, I often set goals where my family might think that I'm starting to go crazy. But setting a goal that may look a bit unreasonable at first feeds me with the needed energy and motivation to be persistent until I reach it. And if I then surround myself with people, such as friends, coaches, and mentors, and learn from their specific knowledge and experience, I gain the certainty over time that my goal is achievable. That's what has been proven to me in so many situations (the Marathon des Sables was one of them), and I'm confident that it will continue to be so. I always prefer to go for ambitious goals, and setting ambitious running goals helped me to improve steadily. Experience proves that missing an ambitious goal by a bit usually leads to a better result than overachieving a modest one. In the end, we're all stronger than we think we are and are capable of shifting the borders of what we believe is possible. But setting ambitious goals is not the same as going for unrealistic ones, and sometimes there's only a thin line separating them. I therefore always attach great importance to finding the right balance between inspiration and managing the mitigation of risks that may lead to failure.

> **When a man does not know what harbor he is making for, no wind is the right wind.**
>
> Seneca

In ultrarunning, there are no shortcuts when it comes to preparation and diligent planning. I doubt anyone would disagree that a lot of training and preparation goes into successfully getting through a race of 100 kilometers or more with thousands of meters of climbing. Every kilometer in training and every strength exercise counts and adds a piece of the puzzle to overall readiness. Knowing that I've done everything possible during preparation to make the planned experience a positive and unique one gives me mental stability. Following a training plan with discipline also helps me to define a concrete goal for the big day itself. I will then, for example, have some important reference points for the timing of my race, my pace. When I ran my first marathons in the early 2000s, I was able to predict my finishing time for the 42.2 kilometers by a couple of minutes because I knew that my preparation was done properly and several test races over shorter distances delivered important target times. Forecasts in running may be somewhat difficult since on race day all can be different, but for me it has worked pretty well. I'm convinced that intermediate goals and proof points deliver important feedback and are essential to success. The skill to be disciplined and committed to a plan has paid off in many situations in my life, particularly in running. I also had to learn that overdoing it with training might turn the whole into the negative. During phases with a super high load in business and much travelling, for example, it has always been important to adapt the training volume as well as eventually reducing my race ambitions.

> Don't judge each day by the harvest you reap
> but by the seeds that you plant.
>
> Robert Louis Stevenson

The Golden Rule tells us to treat other people as we expect to be treated. It has been a guiding principle over a broad range of cultures throughout history. It is mentioned as far back as in the early times of Confucius at around 500 B.C., and it is also a tenet of the world's major religions. The Golden Rule has always had high importance for me in many aspects of my life. It forms an integral part of true comradeship and unselfishness, and there are many stories of ultrarunners sacrificing glory to help out fellow runners in difficult situations. In fact, every runner is even obliged to do so by accepting the regulations of all the big ultra-races in the world. Whenever a fellow runner has a problem, be it an injury or other issue, runners immediately come to help. Personal ambitions move to the background, and the affected runner is then often accompanied over several kilometers by another runner or even a group of runners to ensure that nothing worse happens. Lifelong friendships are often made in such situations. I still remember when I stumbled over a stone and fell down during the Eiger Ultra Trail on the passage towards Schynige Platte in 2014. I did not have a serious injury, but seeing me fall down from the view of the runners behind me must have been a spectacle. Suddenly two of them were with me and only continued on the course after they were assured that I was okay. It is the small but memorable experiences that make this sport what it really is: a haven of comradeship where values are held high, truly. That's why I love it so much!

MERDANI
to
MERZOUGA

STAGE SIX

RUNNING FOR A CAUSE

"I will miss you!"

The sixth and final stage of the Marathon des Sables is called the Charity Stage. It will take us across the dunes of Erg Chebbi, with all of us wearing the same yellow shirts printed with the word Solidarité in red on the front. Although some runners will still focus on time, our little tent community had decided that we would walk across the dunes together. Time isn't added to the overall ranking, though finishing the Charity Stage is mandatory to be ranked.

The Charity Stage allows me to combine my participation in the Marathon des Sables with a purpose that isn't purely personal. Patrick Bauer wrote the following words about the Charity Stage in the roadbook:

"We are lucky to have enough to eat and enjoy the pleasure of running in such beautiful locations. We mustn't forget that there are people around us who need help. And we can do something. The Marathon des Sables solidarity stage is a chance to put the spotlight on the whole charity movement that builds up around Marathon des Sables. Everyone can run or walk hand in hand to make up a marvelous team in the dunes."

Thank you, Patrick, and also for posting my campaign on the Marathon des Sables website.

I will be raising money for Plan International, a global non-governmental organization that advances children's rights and equality for girls. I have been working with Plan International for several years and am also friends with the president of its Swiss chapter, Andreas Buerge. I have committed to a fundraising campaign for clean drinking water in Africa. Water saves lives, and water is life.

I found out later that donated money was used to build a well for clean drinking water in the village of Liati Dafornu in the Volta Region of Ghana. Liati Dafornu is a remote village in the foothills below Mount Afadjato, the highest mountain in Ghana at 885 meters above sea level. The water project included drilling of a well, the construction of hand pumps, and training on how to use and maintain them. Many people in Africa, especially children, suffer because of polluted drinking water, and many die. I concluded my fundraising campaign with a keynote at a Magic Monday event in Zurich in late autumn of 2017. Nearly 100 people attended and helped get the funds to the needed level. Guests not only learned about the works of Plan International but were also spoiled with culinary and musical delights. I was very grateful for the generous donations that evening and all the others, large and small. All helped make Liati Dafornu a better place to live and grow up.

I'm still overwhelmed by the view of the Erg Chebbi dunes. What great cinema! Today we move to the starting area all together one last time. I look around and see only happy faces. What an unbelievable vibe. I can literally feel it!
Patrick speaks for a short time and wishes us good luck on our last 7.7 kilometers. And then the yellow crowd moves. The first 3.5 kilometers are mostly over stony plateaus until we reach the foothills of Erg Chebbi.
For a moment I thought I heard a soft roar. It was like the humming of a cello in the low-frequency range. Was that the singing of the dunes? Unfortunately, the sound had disappeared

as fast as it had come. Was it only my imagination or possibly even some sort of self-fulfilling prophecy whereby I had willed my ears to hear the dunes singing? I'll never know for sure.

The field of runners sticks close together, and as we enter the dunes I can already see the first runners on top of the first ridge. It is an amazing picture and looks almost like a painting in the shimmering early morning light.

I was told that there is a good chance that we will see Tuaregs today, and I am hoping we do. Meanwhile, we reached the top of the first dune, and what a view! Birgit, Markus, Ricarda, Jens, Simon, and I are walking as a group. We're nearly halfway through the stage already. Sliding down the dune hills is terrific, and Ricarda is especially enjoying it.

Then it happens. I see a Tuareg standing atop a dune. I had wished so much to see one in his flowing, indigo-dyed robe, and now there he is, a *targi*, the singular form of a male Tuareg. For a moment I feel I am part of a postcard. How graceful and elegant he looks. The Tuareg are known as the "blue knights of the desert" because their indigo robes often glimmer in the sun. The Tuareg come from the Berbers, and in former times they were nomadic shepherds, but today most live settled lives.

I can already see the finish line at the entrance to the village of Merzouga.

As we approach Merzouga, I start spotting caravans of tourists moving into the dunes, a marked contrast to the isolation we have experienced during our week in the desert. The tourists must have woken up early to be here already. Most are on camels, but I see some tourists heading to the dunes in off-road vehicles. I dislike that: tire tracks mar the beauty of the dunes. Some of the most luxurious tent camps in the Sahara are located here at Erg Chebbi, and we've seen some of them from far off during today's dune crossing. It must be a totally different experience than the one we had in our bivouacs that had only the basic necessities and nothing more for our journey through the desert. But I would choose the way we did it.

Then the big moment comes. I'm officially a finisher of the Marathon des Sables 2017. I've made it. We cross the finish line hand in hand, Birgit, Ricarda, Jens, Markus, Simon, and I. What joy, what an unbelievable moment. Quite a few people are cheering when we arrive. Some are relatives and friends of participants, but I also recognize some tourists as well as locals.

Civilization welcomes us back. The 25 buses that will take us back to Ouarzazate are already lined up and waiting. The drive, about 350 kilometers, will take about 6 hours, including a lunch break somewhere in the open plain. I walk by a big picture of Mohammed VI, the Moroccan king, who has been like a patron saint to us during our journey through the desert. He became king of Morocco in 1999 when he was only 36 years old. One of the richest kings in the world, Mohammed VI is often referred to as *roi des pauvres*, king of the poor, because he mingles with commoners like me.

I arrive at the desert bus depot and board the one I am told to climb into by one of the volunteers. Shortly after our bus drives off, I start the journey with a short power nap – it is probably one of the most deserved naps I have ever taken. The mood on the bus is very relaxed, which is not really a surprise. Finishing the Marathon des Sables, after all, is one of the most significant accomplishments many of us have ever known. It will take me some time to realize what it means, but already I feel like I'm in seventh heaven.

With a time of 39:18:01, I finished in 333rd place out of 1,094 runners. Overall, the experience exceeded all my expectations, and I'm convinced that I will draw mental strength from it for a very long time to come. Our whole tent team finished, which is wonderful. There are always hurdles, many of which could have been impassable, and it can never be taken for granted that you will successfully finish the Marathon des Sables no matter how well prepared you are, and yet we all did. Birgit, Ricarda, Jens, Markus, Simon, and I are together on the bus going back to Ouarzazate. Wow!

After the lunch break we climb back aboard the bus and finally arrive in Ouarzazate in the late afternoon. The Swiss participants are all booked in the same hotel – it is the same one I already spent three nights in before the start of the race. The bus stops in front of the Hotel La Perle du Sud, and I reunite with my duffel bag at reception and receive the key to my room. Like everything during the whole week, all is perfectly organized. My roommate will be Martin Briner, another Swiss runner whom I got to know in early 2017 when we exchanged thoughts on needed supplies and equipment for the race.

I do not know if I have ever taken a longer shower in my life. This is the first one in eight days, and it feels so good. I look at my feet and toes and see that I made it without getting a single blister. Quite astonishing since I had expected that I'd suffer from at least one or more blisters. It seems that my foot-care program in the weeks and months before the race paid off. The anti-chafing sports cream had done its job.

A deep nap is behind me when Martin arrives. We soon head downstairs to an evening made for us. We enjoy food and raise glasses of wine to toast our feat – we did it! – and we toast our triumphs, the challenges bested and our family and friends and our fellowship of runners of the Marathon des Sables; all around is the unmistakable sign that something very special has taken place. Thank you, Patrick Bauer, and the whole team of volunteers for a week that surpassed exceptional!

I enjoy 8 hours of deep sleep. We will spend the day in Ouarzazate, and after a breakfast buffet, my tentmates and I walk the 2 kilometers to the Hotel COS to receive our finisher shirt. The queue is maybe 30 minutes long, and we pass the time chatting with one another. When I get my finisher shirt, I recognize that I probably should have taken one size larger. Medium usually fits me well: I'm 174 centimeters. In this case, a large one would have been the better choice, but since everything needed to be pre-ordered, an exchange is not possible. Oh well, not a problem as long as it does not shrink when washed. I also buy Marathon des Sables-branded shirts and a Buff (I often wear my Buff since my return from the desert, and sometimes I feel like all my Sahara memories are inside it).

The rest of the day is all about lolling around and drinking mint tea while talking about unforgettable moments. There was also an extensive afternoon siesta. The day ends with a last dinner, again in our hotel, offered by the organizer.

I wake up quite early the next day, which tells me that my body is recovering well. It is Easter Sunday, but since Easter is a Christian celebration, there are no signs of it in Ouarzazate. There are no chocolate rabbits or eggs. A driver will take me back over the Atlas Mountains to Marrakech soon after breakfast. It will be a 4-hour drive through one of the most beautiful mountain regions I've ever seen. Habib will await me in his bazaar, where I'll spend a couple of hours in the Medina of Marrakech.

I arrive in Marrakech shortly after noon. My flight will leave at 5:45 p.m., so there is no hurry. Sitting on Habib's rooftop terrace, I fall into a rather sentimental mood. Small pieces of the week in the desert start coming together. I had expected it would be a journey into myself, and that's what it was. When we say goodbye at the bazaar at about 4:00 p.m., Habib has wet eyes, and so do I. We hug and express our hope to see each other soon. "But please bring your family with you next time," Habib says. The spice pack Habib gave me as a gift for the family is safely stowed in my bag. As Habib is engaged with clients, a friend of his drives me to Marrakech's new town of Gueliz, and there I grab a taxi to the airport.

Luggage drop-off, security, and border control are usually a chore, but the airport staff greets all the finishers of the Marathon des Sables as if they are friends. My flight to Basel is on time.

I look out of the window as the plane is climbing and whisper to myself, "Goodbye, Morocco. I will miss you."

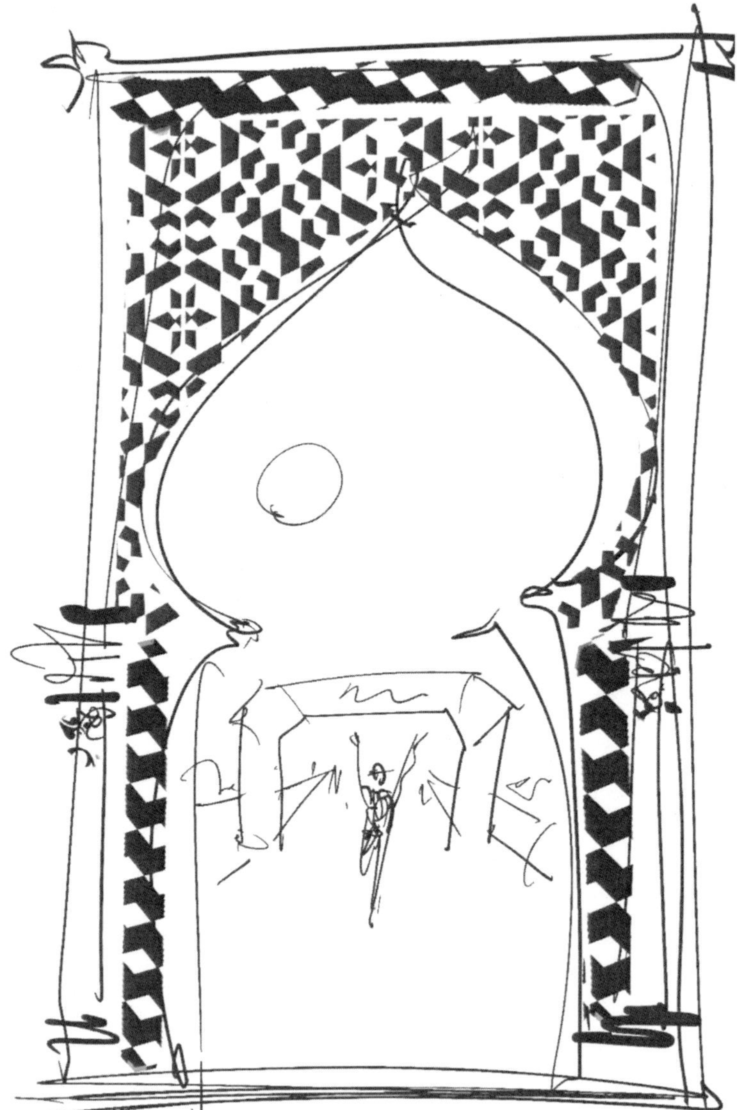

EPILOGUE

I'm sitting on the terrace of our holiday home in Grindelwald and can see the majestic Eiger North Face as I write this epilogue. In the end, it became much more than just a race report about my participation in the 2017 Marathon des Sables. I was also able to capture some important moments in my life, giving it the touch of a memoir at some points.

Running has given me so much over the last 20 years. There must be something deeper about it than just putting on my running shoes and going. Sometimes I feel like nature is calling to me, and I just have to go out, can't resist; it is a feeling that especially overwhelms me when I'm in the mountains. The proximity to nature, which one can literally smell in the mountains, unlike in the big cities, fascinates me. It is not by accident that many of my best running memories, besides the Marathon des Sables, are from when I was in the mountains. When I'm in the mountains around Grindelwald for a long run, it often feels like a kind of meditation. All around me is unspoiled nature. I love the changing colors, the moody mountain weather, the different seasons. When the experience is enriched with the sighting of wildlife, I am overpowered by joy. Chamois, ibexes, marmots, deer, the Swiss Alps are rich with animals that luckily still find a place to live undisturbed.

Running for me also means a deceleration from the pace of my daily life where bad feelings sometimes arise if the day ends with too many open tasks I had planned to finish. When I'm out on the trails, it's all about the next step.

For me, running turned out to be very important in building up my resilience. I believe good leaders should not always be "on." They know how important it is to switch "off" from time to time and fill up their mental energy buckets. You cannot only zap energy. And how is it possible to fill up mental energy buckets on a 100-kilometer or even longer mountain race or while running 237 kilometers through the Moroccan Sahara? For me it mostly happens in phases during runs when I'm in the flow, absorbed by the run, and my mind opens to the world around me, what I am observing, and then I usually also start reflecting on the people in my life and the actions I should take or have taken. Such moments fill up my mental energy buckets as they happen because reflections on life are what give life meaning. And these moments are also like wells that I can return to for refreshment when I need to draw strength.

There have been many running moments over the past 20 years, be it in races or while training, from which I was able to draw a lot of positive energy and optimism for a long time after. From some of them, I still do. The adventure in the Sahara Desert was filled with such moments, and possibly the most outstanding so far, but there have also been many others. The crossing of the finish line at the Ultra Trail du Mont Blanc in 2009 or "flying" down from Scaletta Pass to Dürrboden at one of my seven Swissalpine Marathon completions come to mind; also when I was fighting the moraine after kilometer 40 with the world-famous Eiger, Mönch and Jungfrau mountain trio in front of me at the Jungfrau Marathon, one of the most beautiful marathons in the world according to the Ultimate Guide of Marathons.

I always set a goal first, and I have done that ever since my first marathon in Lausanne. I often feel like I am being pulled toward the goal, and the motivation to successfully reach it gives me all the drive and energy I need. Goals help me focus my attention, and I often use visualization techniques to see myself achieving my plan and goal.

The Marathon des Sables had been a dream for many years, and maybe it was not clearly articulated, but it was always somewhere in the back of my mind. When I started to reflect on what were the important success factors, some things immediately came to mind. Meticulous and diligent preparation is indispensable. Thinking positive in difficult moments and situations is essential and must be practiced before the start of the race. Setting intermediate goals helps to overcome mental barriers and ensures that you get a sense of achievement in the short term. Listening to the body and being aware of any unusual signals from it is also absolutely critical. Support from family is essential, and for me, this was even a *conditio sine qua non*. All my efforts were more than paid back in full, and I am thankful for having had the possibility to participate in that unique event.

I encourage everybody to realize the dreams they hold. Willingness and discipline will shift what you perceive as limits, and you will gain the inspiration and energy you need for the future you see for yourself. As an old Berber saying goes, the person who enters the desert will not be the same one who leaves it. During the week in the desert I developed a different view and perspective on what is important in life. Days and nights in the desert, away from my usual daily life, gave and continue to give me so much.

Marcel Nickler, November 2019

PICTURE MOMENTS

Happy finisher at Swissalpine Marathon 2009 with Monika

In action at Eiger Ultra Trail E51 in 2016

Beautiful Ouarzate, also called the gateway to the desert

The colors and smells of the market in Ouarzazate

My equipment and food consisted of more than 70 individual items

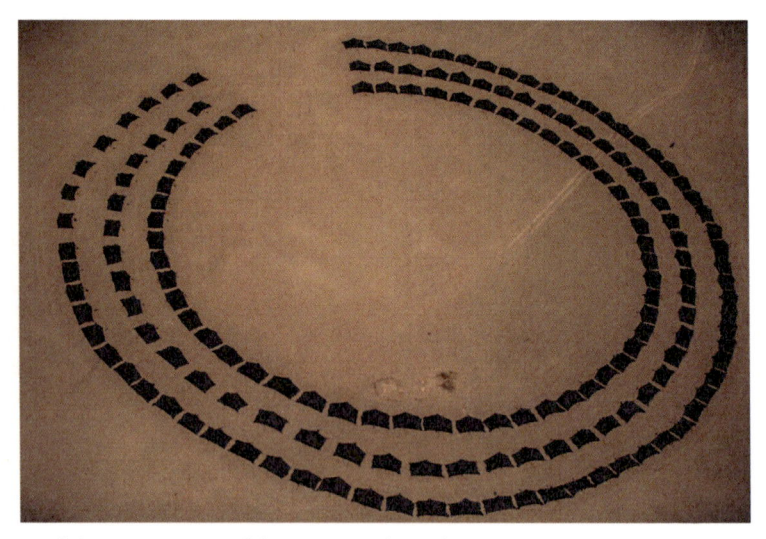

Artful arrangement of the 166 simple Berber tents

The tarpaulin is fixed with wooden poles and iron pegs

Room with a view

The start and finish arch, a true landmark of the daily bivouac

The morning start

Spectacular view from Jebel El Otfal

On a hot passage over a dried-out lake

Checkpoint for time-keeping and water

Race-pack-ready mode in the early morning

The course also included some tough mountain crossings

The M'Fis mining outpost during Stage Four

View of the Erg Chebbi dunes

Lonely runners crossing a dune lake

Like a string of pearls

Fighting the dunes is often hard work

Me, somewhere between meditation and extasy

Our tent number 35 tribe in joyful morning anticipation

EQUIPMENT LIST

Mandatory Equipment

1744 grams

Backpack:	WAA MDS 2017 Ultrabag 20 l with 4-liter front pack
Sleeping bag:	Mammut Sphere Down Spring 180 left
Head torch:	Princeton Tec Remix Pro 200 lumen
Safety pins:	15 pieces
Compass:	Silva Expedition 54 with prism bearing
Lighter:	BIC Mini
Whistle:	integrated in backpack
Knife:	Victorinox Signature with 7 functions
Skin antiseptic:	Kodan tincture forte 6 ml
Hand disinfection:	Sterilium 50 ml
Anti-venom pump:	ASPIVENIN mini suction pump
Signal mirror:	Coglanh's acrylic mirror
Survival sheet:	Aluminum silver/gold
Sun cream:	Daylong extreme 50+
Passport	
Medical certificate:	handed in at check-in
Electrocardiogram:	handed in at check-in
200 Euros in cash:	4x 50 Euros

Marathon-Kit, supplied by the organizers

Roadbook, GPS-Tracker, identification marks, toilet sachets, salt tablets

Clothing and on body

1810 grams

Cap:	RaidLight Sahara Cap
Buff:	Marathon des Sables edition
Socks base layer:	Injinji Liner Crew
Socks:	X Socks Marathon
Running shorts:	Salomon Exo
Running shirt:	X-Bionic The Trick
Underpants:	Uniqlo boxer briefs
Sunglasses:	Julbo Explorer Cameleon
Running shoes:	Brooks Cascadia 10
Desert gaiters:	Raidlight
Watch:	Suunto Ambit2
Windbreaker:	Montane Slipstream GL Jacket
Calves:	Salomon Exo

Clothing, other

436 grams

Armguards:	Montane Via
Spare socks:	X Socks Marathon
Spare underpants:	Uniqlo boxer briefs
Wind protection pants:	Inov-8 ATC Ultra
Shorts (evening):	Nike
Shirt (evening):	F-lite Body Megalight 140

Other Equipment

1101 grams

Water bottles:	WAA MDS 750 ml with pipettes
Sleeping mattress:	Therm-a-Rest NeoAir x-lite S
Inflatable pillow:	Mammut Air Imperial
Safety kit:	Needles, plasters
Cord	
Toilet paper:	7x 6 sheets in zip bag
Wet wipes:	Chamomile scent
Waterproof camera:	Sony TX30 with spare battery
Spork:	Optimus titan spork
Toothbrush:	Maximum white
Teeth cleaning tablets:	Denttabs 7 Mint

Toothpicks:	7 pieces in zip bag
Lip balm:	Mawaii SPF 30
Ultralight bags:	Exped XXS, 3x
Pan:	Toaks Light titanium pot 550 ml
Fuel tablets:	Esbit, 12x 4 g
Stove:	Esbit pocket titanium stove
Cable ties:	8 pieces
Fabric tape	
Repair kit:	Therm-a-Rest
Earplugs:	4 pieces
Slippers:	Lizard RollUp Sandal
Key chain ring:	Wedding ring

FOOD LIST

Day 1: 30.3 km

2854 kcal

Breakfast:	Granola with Raspberries, Expedition Foods
en route:	Peronin Cacao, Treck n'Eat DX2400F (2x), Datrex
Regeneration:	Power Protein, Winforce
Evening:	Macadamia nuts, Sun Queen Chicken Korma with rice, Expedition Foods Beef Jerky, Paleo To Go

Day 2: 39.0 km

2689 kcal

Breakfast:	Porridge with Blueberries, Expedition Foods
en route:	Peronin Cacao, Treck n'Eat DX2400F (2x), Datrex
Regeneration:	Power Protein, Winforce
Evening:	Macadamia nuts, Sun Queen Chicken Tikka with rice, Expedition Foods Beef Jerky, Paleo To Go

Day 3: 31.6 km

2692 kcal

Breakfast:	Porridge with Blueberries, Expedition Foods
en route:	Peronin Cacao, Treck n'Eat DX2400F (2x), Datrex

Regeneration:	Power Protein, Winforce
Evening:	Macadamia nuts, Sun Queen
	Vegetable Tikka with rice, Expedition Foods
	Beef Jerky, Paleo To Go

Day 4: 86.2 km

2932 kcal

Breakfast:	Porridge with Blueberries, Expedition Foods
en route:	Peronin Cacao (2x), Treck n'Eat
	DX2400F (4x), Datrex
Regeneration:	Power Protein (2x), Winforce
Evening:	Macadamia nuts, Sun Queen
	Beef Jerky (2x), Paleo To Go

Day 5: rest day

2545 kcal

Breakfast:	Macaroni and Cheese, Expedition Foods
Regeneration:	Power Protein (2x), Winforce
in between:	Crunchy fruits, foodspring
	Macadamia nuts, Sun Queen
Evening:	Chicken Tikka with rice, Expedition Foods
	Beef Jerky, Paleo To Go

Day 6: 42.2 km

2692 kcal

Breakfast:	Porridge with Blueberries, Expedition Foods
En route:	Peronin Cacao, Treck n'Eat DX2400F (2x), Datrex
Regeneration:	Power Protein, Winforce
Evening:	Macadamia nuts, Sun Queen Vegetable Tikka with rice, Expedition Foods Beef Jerky, Paleo To Go

Day 7 : 7.7 km

2106 kcal

Breakfast:	Porridge with Blueberries, Expedition Foods
En route:	Peronin Cacao, Treck n'Eat Macadamia nuts, Sun Queen

MARATHONS AND MORE

Lausanne Marathon 42.2 km
1999, 2000, 2001, 2002, 2008 Switzerland

My first marathon. Beautiful course along the Lavaux vineyard terraces above the shores of Lake Geneva. You can literally smell the fermenting grapes as you pass through the winemaking villages. Scenic finish line below the famous Olympic Museum.

Hamburg Marathon 42.2 km
2000, 2002, 2004, 2005, 2008 Germany

That's where I did my personal best in the marathon in 2002. Wonderful and atmospheric course through Hamburg's most beautiful areas. A race that is truly close to my heart and one I can recommend to any marathon runner.

Mainz Marathon 42.2 km
2000 Germany

This race consists of two laps through the city of Mainz and its suburbs. Unfortunately, my participation was accompanied by exceedingly high temperatures that I had to pay tribute to.

Jungfrau-Marathon 42.2 km
2000, 2001, 2002, 2003, 2004, 2006, 2007, Switzerland
2008, 2010, 2012, 2013, 2015, 2016

Multiple times awarded the most beautiful marathon in the world by different marathon guides. The second half is difficult but worth the effort. Crossing the finish line makes you feel like a hero. A must-do for every mountain runner.

Paris Marathon 42.2 km
2001 France

The course passes the city's main attractions. I ran it in heavy rain but was a happy finisher, overall. The race is crowded and many runners are in costumes, which seems to be a common thing in France.

Zurich Marathon 42.2 km
2003 Switzerland

Around the lake basin of the Swiss economic capital, one of the most beautiful cities in the world. Flat race and good to run a fast time despite the many tight directional changes in the last kilometers.

Berlin Marathon 42.2 km
2003 Germany

One of the most important and well-known marathons worldwide. Through the city of Berlin, it's a fast course – all the world record marathon times have been set here since 2003.

Swissalpine K78 78.5 km
2005, 2006, 2007, 2008, 2009, 2010, 2012 Switzerland

Awesome course through the valleys around Davos with its legendary summit at Kesch-Hütte. What a pity that the organizer sacrificed this legendary race in favor of a new distance in 2018.

New York Marathon   42.2 km
2006   USA

A must-do for every marathon runner. The race starts on Staten Island and passes by some of New York's most important spots in Brooklyn, Queens, the Bronx and Manhattan. Scenic finish in Central Park. The only marathon I ran with tights.

UTMB   166 km
2009   France, Italy Switzerland

The Ultra-Trail du Mont-Blanc is also known as the summit of trail running. Participants are drawn by lottery, and the reward is a unique course with spectacular mountain views. The runners pass through parts of three different countries.

Swissalpine K42   42.2 km
2011   Switzerland

The little brother of the Swissalpine K78 with the start in Bergün and an immediate ascent up to Kesch-Hütte. Tough course through the beautiful Rhaetian Alps and finish in Davos.

Défi des Seigneurs   73 km
2012, 2013   France

Hilly and demanding course through the Northern Vosges Regional Nature Park with start and finish in Niederbronn-les-Bains. Fantastic landscape in a unique biosphere reserve.

Eiger Ultra Trail E101 101 km
2014, 2015 Switzerland

Launched in 2013, this race has shaken up the European ultrarunning scene. Not much can top the Eiger North Face for inspiration, and runners have splendid views of some of the most beautiful alpine peaks. My favorite.

Eiger Ultra Trail E51 51 km
2016, 2017, 2018 Switzerland

One of the shorter distances offered at the Eiger Ultra Trail that shares part of the course with the E101. After a steep descent from Schynige Platte down to Burglauenen, the route leads straight back to the village of Grindelwald.

Matterhorn Ultraks 46 km
2016 Switzerland

Challenging course through the mountains around Zermatt. The highest point is on Gornergrat at 3,130 meters above sea level, and there are spectacular views of the Matterhorn on the whole course, weather permitting.

Marathon des Sables 237 km
2017 Morocco

Legendary race through the Moroccan Sahara that has taken place since 1986. Fantastic overall experience as detailed in this book. You carry all your equipment and supplies the whole week except for water, which is provided by the organizer. A big dream come true.

Biel Running Days   100 km
2018   Switzerland

This legendary 100 km ultrarunning event took place the first time in 1958. It starts at 10:00 p.m. in the city of Biel. Runners are carried through the night by a unique and mystic atmosphere.

CCC – UTMB   101 km
2018   France, Italy, Switzerland

After an additional loop right after the start in Courmayeur, the race follows the route of the world-famous UTMB with an atmospheric finish in Chamonix. Tough and partly technical course with beautiful views.

Biel Running Days   56 km
2019   Switzerland

The Night-Ultramarathon of Biel, as this race is also called, shares the first 56 km with the legendary 100 km course. A good alternative when the longer distance does not fit into your plans.

ABOUT THE AUTHOR

Marcel Nickler grew up and lives in Switzerland. He has been married for over 33 years to his lovely wife and is the proud father of their two adult daughters. A passionate ultrarunner, he enjoys running in high mountain terrain and also fell in love with the desert during his Marathon des Sables adventure, which forms the heart of this book. Other passions and hobbies include reading, cooking, jazz, and skiing.

In business, Marcel spent the majority of his professional career as a partner at an international management and technology consultancy where his focus was primarily on innovation and digital transformation. Marcel holds several non-executive board positions and invests a substantial part of his time empowering and developing people and teams. He is also regularly engaged in cultural and social affairs. *Running the Sahara* is Marcel's first book.